P9-CLW-571

Kerzner's Project
Management Logic
Puzzles

Kerzner's Project Management Logic Puzzles

By

HAROLD KERZNER, PH.D.

WILEY

John Wiley & Sons, Inc.

Copyright © 2006 by John Wiley & Sons, Inc. All rights reserved

Published by John Wiley & Sons, Inc., Hoboken, New Jersey
Published simultaneously in Canada

No part of this publication may be reproduced, stored in a retrieval system, or transmitted in any form or by any means, electronic, mechanical, photocopying, recording, scanning, or otherwise, except as permitted under Section 107 or 108 of the 1976 United States Copyright Act, without either the prior written permission of the Publisher, or authorization through payment of the appropriate per-copy fee to the Copyright Clearance Center, 222 Rosewood Drive, Danvers, MA 01923, (978) 750-8400, fax (978) 750-4470, or on the web at www.copyright.com. Requests to the Publisher for permission should be addressed to the Permissions Department, John Wiley & Sons, Inc., 111 River Street, Hoboken, NJ 07030, (201) 748-6011, fax (201) 748-6008, or online at http://www.wiley.com/go/permission.

Limit of Liability/Disclaimer of Warranty: While the publisher and author have used their best efforts in preparing this book, they make no representations or warranties with respect to the accuracy or completeness of the contents of this book and specifically disclaim any implied warranties of merchantability or fitness for a particular purpose. No warranty may be created or extended by sales representatives or written sales materials. The advice and strategies contained herein may not be suitable for your situation. You should consult with a professional where appropriate. Neither the publisher nor the author shall be liable for any loss of profit or any other commercial damages, including but not limited to special, incidental, consequential, or other damages.

For general information on our other products and services or for technical support, please contact our Customer Care Department within the United States at (800) 762-2974, outside the United States at (317) 572-3993 or fax (317) 572-4002.

Wiley also publishes its books in a variety of electronic formats. Some content that appears in print may not be available in electronic books. For more information about Wiley products, visit our web site at www.wiley.com.

Library of Congress Cataloging-in-Publication Data:

Kerzner, Harold.
    Kerzner's Project Management Logic Puzzles / by Harold Kerzner.
    p. cm.
    ISBN-13 978-0-471-79346-5 (pbk.)
    ISBN-10 0-471-79346-9 (pbk.)
    1. Project management—Problems, exercises, etc. I. Title.

    HD69.P75K469   2006
    658.4'04--dc22

2005030939

Printed in the United States of America

10 9 8 7 6 5 4 3 2 1

Contents

Preface

More than 20 years ago, on a trip to England, I came across a magazine entitled *Logic Problems*. Over the years I have so enjoyed doing a variety of challenging logic problems and puzzles to the point where I have become addicted and subscribe to several other publications from the same company.

Over the years, I have collected several logic problems that I have found particularly enjoyable and adapted them in project management logic problems. I have used them in my project management courses and seminars and discovered that they can be used as a teaching tool as well. For example, I use Logic Problem #2 to cover the different types of project management contracts. Logic Problems #5 and #7 cover the PMBOK® Guide 2000 version, and Logic Problems #23 to #31 cover the PMBOK® Guide 2004 version. I have used Logic Problems #9, #13, #14, and #63 for the teaching of scheduling techniques. Logic Problems #10 and #63 are helpful in getting students to understand the concepts of earned value measurement systems. Many of the problems come with hints to help you get started, and answers are provided at the end.

More than anything else, these logic problems are enjoyable to do and a form of relaxation, at least for me. For those of you who also enjoy these types of problems and other related logic puzzles, I recommend the magazine *Logic Problems,* from which the idea for many of the problems in this book originated. *Logic Problems* will help you develop and challenge your powers of logical thinking. Each issue comes with step-by-step solutions.

Another magazine that I subscribe to is *Hanjie* magazine. *Hanjie* is a puzzling form of painting by numbers. *Hanjie* means picture puzzle in Japanese, which is where some believe this idea originated. All puzzles are solvable by logic.

For more information on these types of logic puzzles please visit www.puzzler.co.uk.

Harold Kerzner, Ph.D.
Professor of Systems Management
Baldwin-Wallace College
Berea, Ohio 44017

How to Solve
Logic Problems

To solve logic problems, the wording in the clues must be read carefully. All of the necessary information is provided in the clues, and trial-and-error solutions are not necessary. The problems can be solved with simple logic.

Sample Logic Problem:

Three married couples live in three different cities and each couple has a different number of children. The husbands are Alfred, Dirk, and Mickey. The wives are Annette, Barbara, and Cathy but not necessarily married to the husbands according to the order of the husbands' names. The three cities in which the couples live are Boston, Chicago, and Denver, and the numbers of children are one, two and three. In completing the table below, we will use a ● to signify "yes" and an X to signify "no."

Clues:

1. Barbara and Mickey are a couple but do not live in Chicago.
2. One of the couples which does not include Annette live in Boston with their three children
3. Alfred and his wife live in Denver; they have more than one child.
4. Cathy's husband's first name begins with an initial that appears later in the alphabet than Cathy's first-name initial.

Explanation:

From clue 1, Barbara and Mickey are husband and wife. So, a ● can be placed at the intersection and the other cells have an X. Likewise, because they do not live in Chicago, we can place an X in that location as well and any other locations that relate Barbara or Mickey to Chicago. This is shown in the figure below.

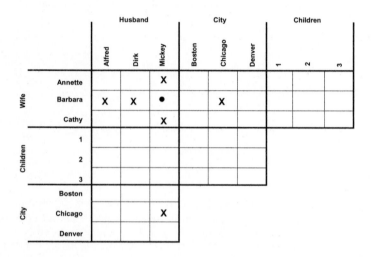

With clue 2, we can signify a "yes" in the box that signifies the intersection of Boston and three children and also a "no" for the Annette location in that column. This is shown below.

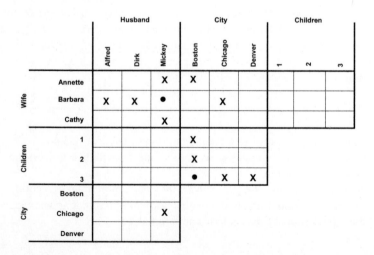

Using clue 3, we can place a "yes" in the intersection of Alfred and Denver, and the corresponding cells will then have a "no" response. We can also eliminate the one child cell from the Alfred row and the Denver column. The result is shown below.

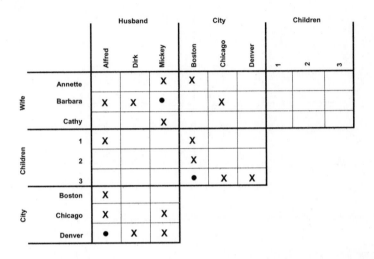

Now notice that in the cells that relate husbands and cities, we know that Dirk must reside in Chicago and Mickey must reside in Boston. Also, Mickey must live in Boston with three children. The results are show below.

		Husband			City			Children		
		Alfred	Dirk	Mickey	Boston	Chicago	Denver	1	2	3
Wife	Annette			X	X					X
	Barbara	X	X	•	•	X	X	X	X	•
	Cathy			X	X					X
Children	1	X	•	X	X	•	X			
	2	•	X	X	X	X	•			
	3	X	X	•	•	X	X			
City	Boston	X	X	•						
	Chicago	X	•	X						
	Denver	•	X	X						

We also know from this figure that the city in which the couple has two children is Denver. This is represented in the figure below.

		Husband			City			Children		
		Alfred	Dirk	Mickey	Boston	Chicago	Denver	1	2	3
Wife	Annette			X	X					X
	Barbara	X	X	•	•	X	X	X	X	•
	Cathy			X	X					X
Children	1	X	•	X	X	•	X			
	2	•	X	X	X	X	•			
	3	X	X	•	•	X	X			
City	Boston	X	X	•						
	Chicago	X	•	X						
	Denver	•	X	X						

Now using clue 4, we know that Cathy cannot be married to Alfred. Therefore, we can complete the figure as shown below.

		Husband			City			Children		
		Alfred	Dirk	Mickey	Boston	Chicago	Denver	1	2	3
Wife	Annette	•	X	X	X	X	•	X	•	X
	Barbara	X	X	•	•	X	X	X	X	•
	Cathy	X	•	X	X	•	X	•	X	X
Children	1	X	•	X	X	•	X			
	2	•	X	X	X	X	•			
	3	X	X	•	•	X	X			
City	Boston	X	X	•						
	Chicago	X	•	X						
	Denver	•	X	X						

We now know the solution to the problem:

- Alfred and Annette live in Denver with two children.
- Mickey and Barbara live in Boston with three children.
- Dirk and Cathy live in Chicago with one child.

Sometimes, you may have to go back over the clues a second or third time to extract more information. However, guessing is never required and logic must prevail.

For other types of logic problems, the difficulty is in knowing which clue or clues to start with. Since this may be more complex, hints are provided to assist you.

Now it's your turn to demonstrate your decision-making skills. Good luck!

Kerzner's Project Management Logic Puzzles

Logic Problem #1: Reports and Reports _____

Three project team members, whose names were Bob, John, and Karen, were assigned the task of preparing the project's performance reports. Each prepared a different report. The three performance reports were a progress report, status report, and forecast report. Each report had a different prognosis after the analysis, namely favorable, neutral, and unfavorable. Each report also had a different number of pages. Using the figure below and the clues, determine who wrote each report, the recommendation from the analysis, and the number of pages.

		Project Manager			Number of Pages			Analysis		
		Bob	John	Karen	3	4	5	Favorable	Neutral	Unfavorable
Type of Report	Progress									
	Status									
	Forecast									
Analysis	Favorable									
	Neutral									
	Unfavorable									
Number of Pages	3									
	4									
	5									

Clues:

1. John's progress report was not five pages in length.
2. Bob's report had a flavor of neutrality in it.
3. The four-page document reported unfavorable results but the five-page forecast report showed favorable results.

Project Manager	Type of Report	Number of Pages	Analysis

Logic Problem #2:
Types of Contracts _____

In the figure below are six different contract types for six different project managers. From the clues under the figure, determine the contract type for each Project Manager and their position in the figure. Knowledge of each type of contract is essential to solve the problem.

Project Manager: Jane; Richard; Paul; Frank; Tim; Alice

Contract Type: Cost-Plus-Percentage-of-Cost (CPPC); Firm-Fixed-Price (FFP); Cost-Plus-Incentive-Fee (CPIF); Fixed-Price-Incentive-Fee (FPIF); Cost-Plus-Fixed-Fee (CPFF); Time & Materials (T&M)

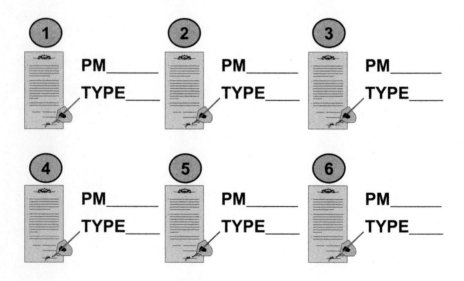

Clues:

1. The contract type, which today is illegal in the government, is located in position 4 in the diagram.
2. Tim's project has a contract that contains a "ceiling" and "floor" on profits.
3. Alice's contract is in an even-numbered position in the diagram.
4. The two incentive-type contracts are located in different rows in the figure and horizontally adjacent to only one other contract, and both of the adjacent contracts are for projects managed by female Project Managers.
5. Frank's project, which is not in position 3, and Richard's project are not adjacent to each other either horizontally or vertically and are located in different rows.
6. The contract type with the maximum risk exposure to the seller is to the right (as you look at the figure) and next to the Cost-Plus contract, where the fee is defined as a dollar value rather than as a percentage, and above the contract type that contains a point-of-total-assumption term.

Logic Problem #3: Redesigning a Component _____

Andrea, the executive sponsor for the project, needed to get a critical problem resolved. A piece of equipment had just failed and a new design had to be developed. She convened a team of four of her project team members, whose names were Bob, Fred, Henry, and Louis, to analyze a piece of equipment that had failed. The team members are in positions 1–4 in the figure below. Each person had a different set of skills to bring to the problem-solving session, which was to find the cause of the failure and redesign the component. Each had a different title and had worked on project teams for a different number of years.

The team successfully identified the problem and redesigned the component with Andrea and three of the four team members agreeing with the new design. The person on the right (i.e., the grouch), who never trusts anyone else's solution except his own, seemed unhappy that someone else's design other than his was accepted by the group.

From the clues below, identify the position of each person in the figure, their name and title, and the number of years they had been working on project teams. Note: Assume that left and right are as you look at the figure below.

Name: Bob; Fred; Henry; Louis (Andrea is on the left, of course)

Title: Project Manager; Assistant Project Manager; Electrical Engineer; Mechanical Engineer

Years of Experience: 10 years; 14 years; 17 years; 21 years

Name ___ ___   ___ ___
Title ___ ___   ___ ___
Years ___ ___   ___ ___

Clues:

1. Fred, the Electrical Engineer, is standing somewhere to the left of the person who has 10 years of experience.
2. Louis, who is not standing next to Bob, is shown standing further to the right in the figure than the Project Manager.
3. The person with 14 years of experience is standing in position 3 in the figure.
4. The Mechanical Engineer is standing immediately to Henry's left.
5. The number of years of experience of the Assistant Project Manager is a prime number.

Hint: If you need help, another clue can be found on p. 195.

Logic Problem #4:
The Unfortunate Overruns _____

Five Project Managers were sitting together at lunch discussing their cost overruns. From the figure below and the accompanying clues, identify the full name of each Project Manager, the reason for their cost overrun, and the size of each Project Manager's cost overrun.

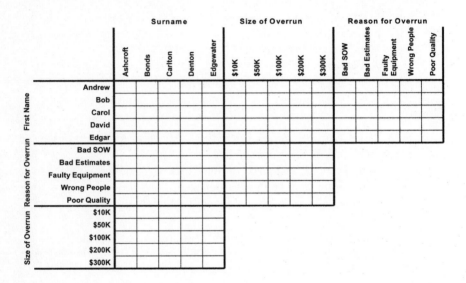

Clues:

1. None of the Project Managers have the same initial for their first and last names.
2. David Carlton's overrun, which was not $100K, was the result of poor estimates by the engineering managers.
3. Ashcroft spent more than one hour complaining about her $200K overrun.
4. One of the Project Managers complained about a $50K cost overrun resulting from the wrong people being assigned to the project.
5. Andrew Edgewater's overrun was larger than Carlton's overrun.
6. Bob's overrun was larger than Edgewater's overrun by more than $100K.
7. Bonds complained about having an overrun resulting from poor quality.
8. The bad Statement of Work (SOW) did not create the largest cost overrun, and the $200K overrun was not the result of faulty equipment.

First Name	Surname	Overrun Reason	Overrun Size

Logic Problem #5:
Training People in the
PMBOK® Guide 2000

Five Project Managers were each asked to set up an internal training program for the company covering certain PMBOK® Guide Areas of Knowledge. The five knowledge areas where trainers were needed were Scope Management, Time Management, Cost Management, Risk Management, and Communications Management. Using the figure below and the accompanying clues, determine the full name of each Project Manager, the knowledge area they chose to teach, and the number of hours they needed for their module. (Note: This problem requires knowledge of the inputs, tools and techniques, and outputs of certain 2000 PMBOK® Guide Areas of Knowledge.)

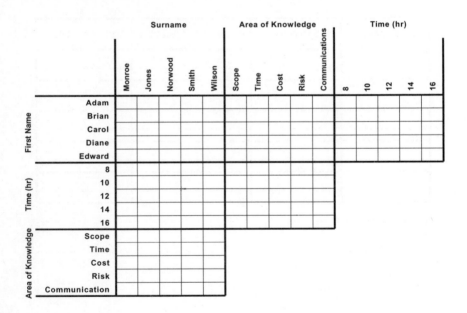

Clues:

1. Brian Jones selected the module where the Work Breakdown Structure (WBS) was neither an input nor an output of any of the processes in any of the knowledge areas.
2. Wilson selected the only module where constraints and assumptions were neither an input nor an output of any of the processes in that knowledge area.
3. The largest number of hours was assigned to Cost Management.
4. Norwood's knowledge area discussed the project charter as either an input or an output.
5. Edward selected the only module where lesson learned was neither an input nor an output to any of the processes.
6. One of the Project Managers complained that 10 hours might not be enough for her area of knowledge.
7. Adam and Carol had areas of knowledge where assumptions and constraints appeared three times as either inputs or outputs to the processes.
8. The module with the greatest number of processes required eight hours of training time.

First Name	Surname	Knowledge Area	Time Needed

Logic Problem #6: Rewarding Project Team Members _____

Once a year, Kramer Industries selects employees to receive awards for exemplary performance on project teams. This year, five people were selected: one from Project Management, Accounting, Quality, Engineering, and Manufacturing. Kramer Industries believed in providing nonmonetary awards rather than cash awards. The nonmonetary awards were a gift certificate for dinner at an exclusive restaurant, theatre tickets, tickets to a sports event, use of a company car for a week, and two days of management-granted time off. Each person also received a gift certificate for one item from the company's gift catalog. The catalog gift certificates were colored red, green, yellow, blue, and purple. From the clues below, determine the title of each person and which two awards each person received.

		Project Team Members					Catalog Gifts					Other Gifts				
		PM	Accountant	Quality	Engineering	Manufacturing	Red	Green	yellow	Blue	Purple	Dining	Theatre	Sports	Company Car	Time Off
Name	Bill															
	Frank															
	Gerald															
	Norman															
	Melissa															
Other Gifts	Dining															
	Theatre															
	Sports															
	Company Car															
	Time Off															
Catalog Gifts	Red															
	Green															
	Yellow															
	Blue															
	Purple															

Clues:

1. Frank was awarded the purple gift certificate for a catalog purchase.
2. Gerald received tickets to a sports event.
3. Norman did not receive use of the company car, which was not paired up with the red catalog gift certificate.
4. The representative from the Quality Division was delighted to receive the gift certificate for dinner at an elegant restaurant.
5. The Project Manager received the blue gift certificate for a catalog purchase.
6. The person from the Engineering Division, who had previously complained that she had never won an award, did not receive the green gift certificate for the catalog purchase or the yellow gift certificate that was paired up with the theatre tickets, which were not awarded to the Accountant.
7. Norman is not from Manufacturing.

Name	Title	Catalog Gift	Other Gift

Logic Problem #7: Understanding the Domain Areas _____

The Wisdom Book Publisher has just published a set of six books, each discussing one of the six PMBOK® Guide Domain Areas: Initiation, Planning, Execution, Control, Closure, and Professional Responsibility. The cover of each book has a different color and each book has a different number of pages. The figure below shows the books, as they would be lying flat on a desk.

Book: Initiation; Planning; Execution; Control; Closure; Professional Responsibility

Color: Red; Yellow; Green; White; Purple; Black

Number of pages: 80; 90; 95; 100; 105; 120

Position	Domain	Color	Pages
1	____	____	____
2	____	____	____
3	____	____	____
4	____	____	____
5	____	____	____
6	____	____	____

Using the clues below, determine the domain area, color, and number of pages for each book.

Clues:

1. The book with the yellow cover is in position 5.
2. The book in position 2 has more pages than the book in position 4.
3. The book with 105 pages is in position 3. The other book with an odd number of pages is in either position 1 or position 2.
4. The book with the most number of pages references only two areas of knowledge in the PMBOK® Guide, and the cover of the book is not red.
5. The books discussing the Execution and Closure domain areas are side by side and both have an even number of pages, but neither book has a green cover.
6. The book discussing the Professional Responsibility domain area has a white cover and is not adjacent to either the purple-colored cover or the black-colored cover, which has an odd number of pages.
7. The domain area that references the fewest PMBOK® Guide Areas of Knowledge is in position 2 in the figure.
8. The book discussing the Planning domain area is at one end of the stack and the book discussing the Control domain area is at the other end.
9. The number of pages in the book in position 1 is greater than the number of pages in the book in position 6 by more than 10 pages.

Hint: If you need help, another clue appears on p. 195. Also, an understanding of p. 38 of the 2000 PMBOK® Guide is essential. For this problem, do not consider the number of areas of knowledge related to the Professional Responsibility domain area since it is not included on p. 38 of the 2000 PMBOK® Guide.

Logic Problem #8:
The PMO Organizational
Structure _____

A company has just set up a Project Management Office (PMO). Eight people are assigned to the PMO and each has a unique responsibility within the PMO. The organizational chart for the PMO is shown below.

Name: John; Florence; Karen; Mollie; Nellie; Roger; Thomas; William

Responsibility: PMO Manager; Six Sigma Monitoring; Benchmarking; PM Tools; Project Management Methodology (EPM); Mentorship; Project Management Information System (PMIS); Portfolio Management of Projects

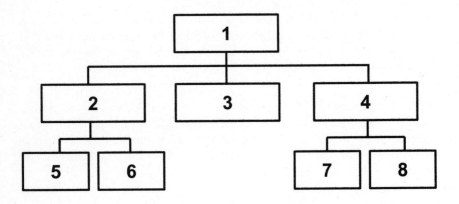

Position	Name	Responsibility
1	____	_____
2	____	_____
3	____	_____
4	____	_____
5	____	_____
6	____	_____
7	____	_____
8	____	_____

Using the clues below, determine the name and responsibility assigned to each position.

Clues:

1. Position 1 is naturally the Manager of the PMO.
2. As you look at the figure, there is nobody positioned to the left of Florence, who is not responsible for PMIS, or William.
3. The person responsible for Six Sigma, which is not John's area of expertise, and Mentorship are in the bottom row.
4. Nellie, Karen (who is responsible for EPM), and Roger (who is responsible for PM Tools) have people positioned to their left and right as you look at the organizational chart.
5. Thomas is assigned to position 4.
6. John and the woman responsible for Benchmarking report to the person in position 2.
7. Position 1 is a male but position 2 and position 3 are females.

Hint: If you need help, another clue appears on p. 195.

Logic Problem #9:
The Mysterious
Network Diagram _____

A Project Manager discovers that his team has neglected to complete the network diagram for the project. The network diagram is shown below. However, the Project Manager has some information available, specifically that each activity, labeled A–G, has a different duration between one and seven weeks. Also, the slack time for each of the activities is known as shown below.

Duration (weeks):   1, 2, 3, 4, 5, 6, 7
Slack time (weeks):   0, 0, 0, 2, 4, 4, 7

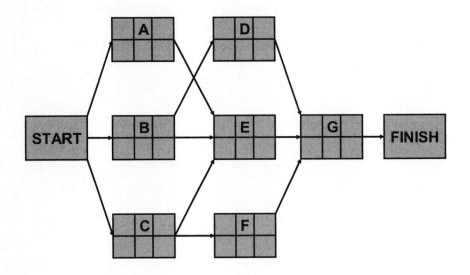

Using the clues provided below, determine the duration of each activity as well as the early start (ES), early finish (EF), latest start (LS), and latest finish (LF) times for each activity.

Clues:

1. Activity E is on the critical path.
2. The ES for activity F is 5 weeks.
3. The duration of activity B is 7 weeks.
4. Activity D has 4 weeks of slack, but activity F has a greatest amount of slack.
5. The EF for activity G is 17 weeks.
6. The LF for activity E is 13 weeks.

Activity	Duration	Early Start	Early Finish	Latest Start	Latest Finish
A	_____	_____	_____	_____	_____
B	_____	_____	_____	_____	_____
C	_____	_____	_____	_____	_____
D	_____	_____	_____	_____	_____
E	_____	_____	_____	_____	_____
F	_____	_____	_____	_____	_____
G	_____	_____	_____	_____	_____

Logic Problem #10:
The Incomplete Status
Report _____

As a continuation of Logic Problem #9, you also discover that the status report for your project is somewhat incomplete. The status report is shown below. From the clues provided, complete the status report.

Clues:

1. For activity B, PV = $100.
2. For activity C, EV = $200.
3. For activity D, AC = $300.
4. Activity A has not started yet.
5. For all of the activities EV (Total) = $930.

Activity	PV	EV	AC	SV	CV
A	_____	_____	_____	($100)	0
B	_____	_____	_____	50	60
C	_____	_____	_____	60	60
D	_____	_____	_____	100	80
E	_____	_____	_____	120	(20)
	======	======	=======	======	=====
Total	_____	_____	_____	_____	_____

Logic Problem #11:
Project Failures _____

Five Project Managers who were attending a local PMI Chapter meeting were all sitting around the same table. Each one complained about their project and the fact that it was failing. From the clues provided below, determine the first and last names of each Project Manager, whom their customer was, and the reason why their project was failing.

Clues:

1. Carlton was managing the project for Epsilon Company.
2. Natalie, whose surname is not Richardson (which happens to be the person with the 300 percent cost overrun), was complaining about the trouble she was having managing the Alpha Company project.
3. No Project Manager has the same initial for the start of his or her first and last name. Also, Barry's customer did not start with the letter "B."
4. The Delta Company Project Manager could not stop complaining about the faulty Statement of Work (SOW) that was provided by the customer.
5. Bellows, whose first name is not Denise, did not have faulty equipment on his project and was not managing the Gamma Company project.
6. Barry complained that he might lose his job because the customer was furious over the poor quality (or lack of it) on his project.
7. Franklin's first name does not have the letter "R" in it. Franklin's complaint was that her company had a shortage of resources that could be assigned to projects and people with the necessary skills were not being assigned.
8. Denise Carlton was pleased to know that she was not the only person whose project was in trouble.
9. Anthony and Bellows argued as to whose project was in worse shape.

	Surname					Customer					Reason for Failure				
	Ashcroft	Bellows	Carlton	Franklin	Richardson	Alpha Co.	Beta Co.	Delta Co.	Epsilon Co.	Gamma Co.	Bad SOW	Cost Overrun	Faulty Equipment	No People	Quality
First Name Anthony															
Barry															
Denise															
Larry															
Natalie															
Reason for Failure Bad SOW															
Cost Overrun															
Faulty Equipment															
No People															
Quality															
Customer Alpha Co.															
Beta Co.															
Delta Co.															
Epsilon Co.															
Gamma Co.															

First Name	Surname	Customer	Reason for Failure

Logic Problem #12:
The Training Programs _____

The International Institute for Learning conducts a Project Management Certification Training Program in three sessions, each session separated by about one month: session I, Integration Management, Scope Management, and Time Management; session II, Cost Management, Risk Management, and Human Resources Management; and session III, Procurement Management, Quality Management, Communications Management, and Professional Responsibility.

Most Project Managers attend the same city for all three sessions. However, five Project Managers discovered that, because of workloads and project requirements, they were not able to attend all three sessions in the same city. From the clues below, identify in which cities each of the five Project Managers attended the three sessions. Also, with everything else being equal, which Project Manager appears to have accumulated the greatest amount of frequent flier miles?

Clues:

1. Each Project Manager (PM) went to a different city for each of the three sessions and none of the PMs were in the same city at the same time. But each PM took the sessions in order, namely, session I, then session II, and finally session III.
2. None of the PMs either lived in or went to a city that had the same starting letter as their surname.
3. Bellows attended session II in Denver but did not attend session I in Los Angeles.
4. The PM who learned about the Probability Impact Matrix in Los Angeles flew to Denver for the next session.
5. The PM who attended session I in Chicago traveled east for sessions II and III, but not necessarily to the nearest city first.
6. One PM traveled from his home in Chicago to Pittsburgh to learn about Professional Responsibility.
7. Each PM attended session I in their home city.
8. The PM who learned about Scope Management in Boston learned about Communications Management in Chicago.
9. Andrews learned about Time Management in Chicago.

		Project Manager					Session III					Session II				
		Andrews	Bellows	Carlton	Daily	Lyndhurst	Boston	Pittsburgh	Chicago	Denver	Los Angeles	Boston	Pittsburgh	Chicago	Denver	Los Angeles
Session I	Boston															
	Pittsburgh																
	Chicago																
	Denver																
	Los Angeles																
Session II	Boston																
	Pittsburgh																
	Chicago																
	Denver																
	Los Angeles																
Session III	Boston																
	Pittsburgh																
	Chicago																
	Denver																
	Los Angeles																

PM	Session I	Session II	Session III

Logic Problem #13: Another Mysterious Network Diagram

A Project Manager discovers that his team has neglected to complete the network diagram for the project. The network diagram is shown below. However, the Project Manager has some information available, specifically that each activity, labeled A-G, has a different duration between one and seven weeks. Also, the slack time for each of the activities is known as shown below.

Duration (weeks):   1, 2, 3, 4, 5, 6, 7
Slack time (weeks):   0, 0, 0, 1, 1, 3, 7

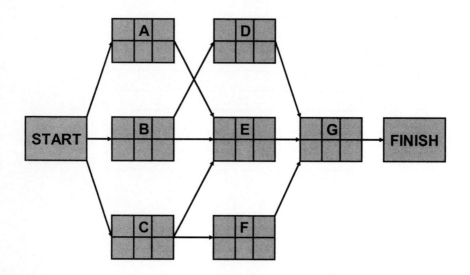

Using the clues provided below, determine the duration of each activity as well as the early start (ES), early finish (EF), latest start (LS), and latest finish (LF) times for each activity.

Clues:

1. Activity E is the longest duration activity and is on the critical path, which is the unlucky number 13; also, there is only one critical path.
2. The EF for activity F is 11 weeks.
3. The LS for activity D is 9 weeks.
4. If activity A slips by 1 week, it will be on a critical path.

Activity	Duration	Early Start	Early Finish	Latest Start	Latest Finish
A	_____	_____	_____	_____	_____
B	_____	_____	_____	_____	_____
C	_____	_____	_____	_____	_____
D	_____	_____	_____	_____	_____
E	_____	_____	_____	_____	_____
F	_____	_____	_____	_____	_____
G	_____	_____	_____	_____	_____

Logic Problem #14:
Yet Another Mysterious
Network Diagram _____

A Project Manager discovers that his team has neglected to complete the network diagram for the project. The network diagram is shown below. However, the Project Manager has some information available, specifically that each activity, labeled A–G, has a different duration between one and seven weeks. Also, the slack time for each of the activities is known as shown below.

Duration (weeks):   1, 2, 3, 4, 5, 6, 7
Slack time (weeks):   0, 0, 0, 3, 6, 8, 8

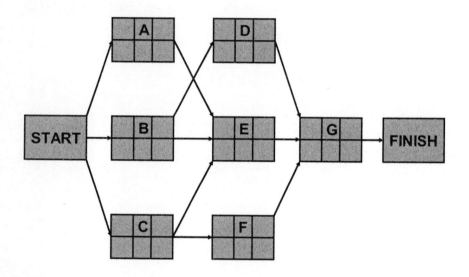

Using the clues provided below, determine the duration of each activity as well as the early start (ES), early finish (EF), latest start (LS), and latest finish (LF) times for each activity.

Clues:

1. There exists only one critical path and it is the largest possible number given the possible durations shown.
2. Activity E has the smallest amount of slack that is greater than zero.
3. The EF for activity A is four weeks and this does not equal the LF. (Note: There is no negative slack in the network.)
4. The slack in activity C is eight weeks.
5. The duration of activity F is greater than the duration of activity C by at least two weeks.

Activity	Duration	Early Start	Early Finish	Latest Start	Latest Finish
A	_____	_____	_____	_____	_____
B	_____	_____	_____	_____	_____
C	_____	_____	_____	_____	_____
D	_____	_____	_____	_____	_____
E	_____	_____	_____	_____	_____
F	_____	_____	_____	_____	_____
G	_____	_____	_____	_____	_____

Logic Problem #15: Congratulating the New PMPs®

Acme Company was delighted when it found out that several of its employees had decided to become PMPs®. To show the company's appreciation, one of the walls in the cafeteria was labeled the "Wall of Fame," upon which would be hung the pictures of each person that passed the exam along with their name and their functional organization.

Seven employees (three men and four women) passed the exam. The names of the people that passed the exam and the functional groups to which they were assigned are shown below. Each person who passed the exam comes from a different department.

Employee: Alice; Daniel; Hilda; Kenneth; Nadine; Olive; Steven
Department: Engineering; Manufacturing; R&D; Sales; Marketing; Accounting; Information Systems

Using the clues below and the figure beneath the clues, position the employees and their functional group with each of the pictures.

Clues:

1. The employee in picture 3 is Kenneth.
2. The picture of the woman from Marketing is at one end of the row.
3. Olive's picture is immediately beside that of Daniel, who does not work in Sales.
4. Nadine's picture is two positions to the right of the person who works in Accounting.
5. Picture 5 represents the Information Systems Department.

6. Hilda works in Manufacturing and her picture is positioned somewhere to the right of Steven's picture.
7. The person from Engineering occupies an odd-numbered position in the row of pictures.
8. The man represented in picture 6 does not work in R&D.

Hint: If you need help, another clue appears on p. 195.

Wall of Fame

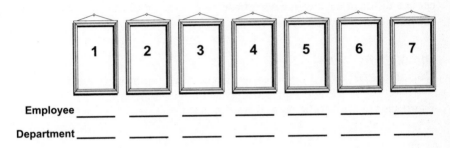

Employee _____ _____ _____ _____ _____ _____ _____

Department _____ _____ _____ _____ _____ _____ _____

Logic Problem #16:
Six Sigma Achievement
Awards _____

With the success in recognizing the accomplishment of the workers in becoming PMPs®, Acme Company decided to dedicate another wall in the cafeteria to those individuals that had successfully implemented Six Sigma projects. Four Black Belt Project Managers successfully completed projects, each project in a different engineering department. Also, each project saved the company a different amount of money.

Black Belt: Amos; Barry; Carol; Denise
Department: Civil Engineering; Electrical Engineering; Industrial Engineering; Mechanical Engineering
Savings: $100K; $200K; $500K; $1M

    Using the clues below and the figure, determine the name of the Black Belt Project Manager in each picture, the department where the Six Sigma project took place, and the amount of money saved with the implementation of each Six Sigma project.

Clues:

1. The picture with the $500K cost savings in the Mechanical Engineering Department is shown immediately to the left of Barry's picture.
2. The $200K cost savings appears immediately to the right of the picture of Amos.
3. None of the initials of the first names of the Project Managers match the letter indicating their position on the wall.

4. Carol saved the company $100K with the successful implementation of her project. She is positioned further to the left on the wall than the picture representing the Civil Engineering Department.
5. Denise managed the project for the Electrical Engineering Department.
6. Position 2 on the wall does not represent the successfully completed project in the Industrial Engineering Department.

Hint: If you need help, another clue appears on p. 195.

Wall of Fame

Black Belt _____   _____   _____   _____

Department _____   _____   _____   _____

Savings _____   _____   _____   _____

Logic Problem #17: A Problem with Procurement _____

Eight Project Managers had ordered small quantities of raw materials for their projects. Eight packages arrived with the raw materials for each of the Project Managers. Each package was wrapped in a different-colored paper. The packages were placed on two tables as shown in the figure below. Using the clues below, identify which package belongs to which Project Manager and the color of the wrapping paper of each package.

Project Manager: Andrea; Barbara; Charlie; David; Edward; Francine; Gwen; Harry

Wrapping Paper: Beige; Black; Blue; Brown; Green; Pink; White; Yellow

Clues:

1. Francine's package and the yellow package are on table 1; Francine's package is positioned immediately to the left of the yellow package.
2, The package wrapped in black paper is in position 8.
3. Gwen's package, which is next to Harry's package and on the same table, is wrapped in beige paper and occupies an odd-numbered position.
4. Edward's package is immediately bordered by the package wrapped in pink and the package wrapped in brown paper, the latter being in a position numbered three higher or lower than the package with white wrapping paper.
5. The package in position 6 belongs to David; one of his immediate neighbors is the package wrapped in blue, while the package wrapped in green is on the other table positioned next to Barbara's package.

6. Andrea's position in the figure has a lower number than Charlie's position, the latter not being in a corresponding position with that of Francine's package on the other table.

Hint: If you need help, another clue appears on p. 195.

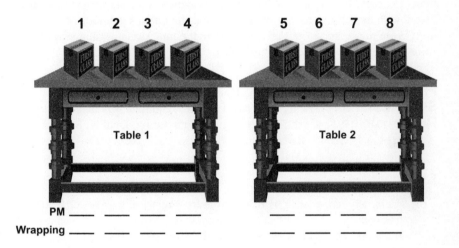

Logic Problem #18: Briefing the Team _____

The Project Manager decided to brief his six team members on the organizational structure for the project. The six team members are shown in the figure below with their backs to you. (Note: left and right are as you look at the figure.) From the clues below, determine the first name, surname, and area of responsibility of each of the team members.

First Name: David; Frank; Jeanie; Naomi; Paula; Steven
Surname: Dante; Edwards; Gamble; Jennings; Newman; Springer
Responsibility: Cost; Engineering; Manufacturing; Quality; Safety; Software

Clues:

1. Paula, who happens to be responsible for engineering, is seated next to Jennings.
2. Team member C is David, but team member B is not Naomi.
3. The team member responsible for cost is seated immediately to the left of Jeanie and immediately to the right of Edwards.
4. Team member E is responsible for software but team member A is not responsible for quality.
5. Team member D is Newman, but the team member named Springer is not in position F.
6. The team member responsible for safety is seated next but one to the right of Dante.
7. Gamble, who has the responsibility for all of manufacturing, is seated next but one on either the left or right of Steven.

Hint: If you need help, another clue appears on p. 195.

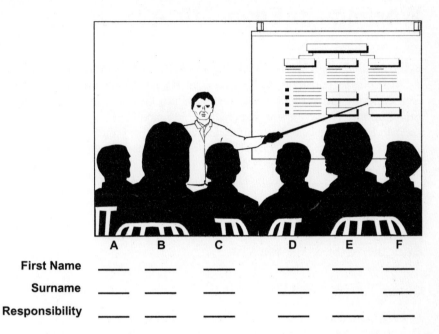

	A	B	C	D	E	F
First Name	___	___	___	___	___	___
Surname	___	___	___	___	___	___
Responsibility	___	___	___	___	___	___

Logic Problem #19:
Who Sits in Each Office? _____

Sitting in the Project Management Office (PMO) are four Project Managers.
 Their offices, namely A, B, C, and D, are along the same wall and all of
their desks are facing in the same direction. Each Project Manager is a different pay grade. The pay grades are grades 6, 7, 8, and 9.
 Each Project Manager has a different budget for his project. The budgets
are $2M, $3M, $4M, and $5M. The pay grades for the Projects Managers are
not related to the size of their budgets. Using the clues below, determine the
name, pay grade, and project budget for each Project Manager.

Name: Adams; Bellows; Caruso; Davidson
Grade: 6; 7; 8; 9
Budget: $2M; $3M; $4M; $5M

Clues:

1. Davidson's office is immediately in front of the grade 6.
2. Caruso's office is immediately ahead of the grade 7, whose project
   budget is not $4M.
3. Both Adams's office and the office of the grade 8 are somewhere in
   front of the Project Manager with a $3M budget.
4. The office of the grade 9 Project Manager is further back than the Project Manager with the smallest budget, who is not in office C.
5. Bellows is the Project Manager with the largest budget.

Hint: If you need help, another clue appears on p. 195.

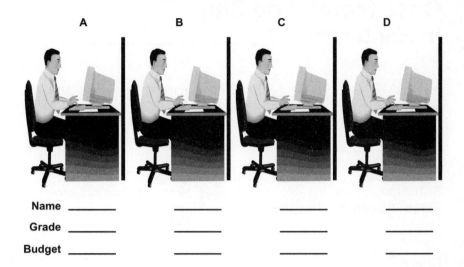

	A	B	C	D
Name	_____	_____	_____	_____
Grade	_____	_____	_____	_____
Budget	_____	_____	_____	_____

Logic Problem #20:
Once More! Who Sits
in Each Office? _____

A Project Manager and three Assistant Project Managers who just happen to be engineers sit in adjacent offices, as shown in the figure below. From the clues below, determine the name and title of each person and the office in which they reside.

First Name: Alicia; Bob; Charles; Denise
Surname: Manning; Newton; Parson; Robinson
Titles (according to rank):   Project Manager; Senior Engineer;
                         Engineer; Junior Engineer

Clues:

1. The office of the Junior Engineer is somewhere to the right of Bob's office but not necessarily adjacent.
2. Robinson is the Project Manager and considered to be senior to all of the engineers.
3. The person in office D is senior to Alicia but junior in rank to Manning, who does not occupy office A in the diagram.
4. The office of Mr. Newton is adjacent to Denise's office.

Hint: If you need help, another clue appears on p. 195.

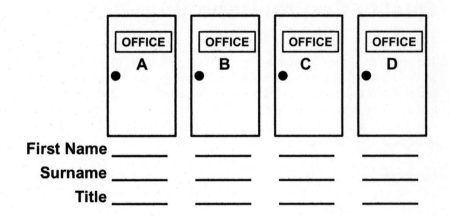

First Name _____ _____ _____ _____

Surname _____ _____ _____ _____

Title _____ _____ _____ _____

Logic Problem #21:
Quality Control Reporting _____

The president of the company has decided that posting the monthly quality control reports for each project might motivate the workers to improve their performance, especially with regard to quality. The figure below shows a bulletin board on which are posted the monthly quality reports from seven projects. Using the clues below, determine the project associated with each of the quality control reports in the figure.

Reports: Phoenix Project; Low Texture Project; Red Prism Project; Blue Spectrum Project; Low Density Project; Spiral Project; Poltex Project

Clues:

1. The Blue Spectrum report is positioned between and on the same line as the Low Density report and the Poltex report.
2. Report 1, which has a one-word title, is not the Phoenix report.
3. The Low Texture report is positioned next to and on the same row as a project with a one-word title.
4. The Spiral report is positioned on the same row and immediately to the right of the Red Prism report.

Hint: If you need help, another clue appears on p. 195.

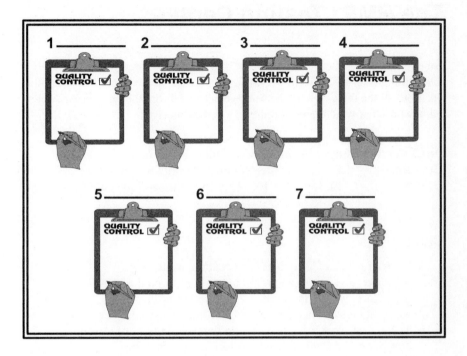

Logic Problem #22:
The PMP® Testing Center _____

On one fine sunny day, six participants, three men and three women, entered the testing center for the PMP® Certification exam. In the figure below are the positions of the tables where the tests were given. From the clues below, determine who sat at which table and the scores they received.

First name: Edgar; Frieda; Howard; Julie; Rose; Tom
Surname: Kipple; Lancaster; Monroe; North; Oswald; Pierce
Score: 140; 150; 160; 165; 170; 180 (all scores are out of 200 points with 137 as passing)

Clues:

1. None of the rows have three men or three women.
2. Kipple received as score of 150 but did not sit on the right-hand side.
3. Mrs. North was sitting to the immediate left of Pierce.
4. Rose sat between two people whose combined scores were 330.
5. The lowest score was the person in the table in front of Oswald.
6. Tom sat in the front row and received a score of 165.

Hint: If you need help, another clue appears on p. 195.

First Name _____	
Surname _____	
Score _____	

EXAM MONITOR

Logic Problem #23:
Integration Management
(PMBOK® Guide 2004) _____

Five Project Managers were assigned the responsibility of teaching the first five sections of the Integration Management chapter in the PMBOK® Guide 2004. Each Project Manager taught a different process, required a different amount of time for teaching, and created a different number of multiple-choice questions as a review. Using the clues and the figure below, determine which Project Manager taught each process, the time required, and the number of review questions.

Note: Knowledge of this chapter in the PMBOK® Guide 2004 is required to do this problem. Although there are seven sections to Integration Management, do not consider the last two sections of the Integration Management chapter when doing this problem.

Clues:

1. Maggie taught one of the two processes that describe four tools and techniques; she required two hours to teach the subject and used an exam with 12 questions.
2. The lecture of 2.5 hours was for a process where the project charter was an input.
3. Five test questions and eight test questions were used in the two processes where either the statement of work or scope statement was not an input, although not necessarily in this order.
4. Quinton taught for 2.5 hours on the only process where the scope statement was an output.
5. Alfonso taught the only process where expert judgment was not part of the tools and techniques and used three hours to teach the material.
6. Susan taught one of the two processes where enterprise environmental factors were not an input.
7. The eight-question test accompanied a 1.5-hour lecture for a process where organizational process assets were not an input; this was not the section on process execution.
8. Ten questions were not used in the process involving monitoring and control.

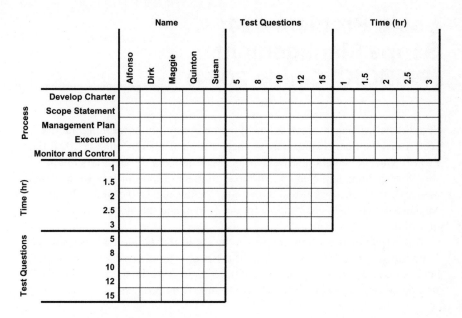

Project Manager	Process	Number of Questions	Time (hr)

Logic Problem #24: Scope Management (PMBOK® Guide 2004) _____

Five Project Managers were assigned the responsibility of teaching the five sections of the Scope Management chapter in the PMBOK® Guide 2004. Each Project Manager taught a different process, required a different amount of time for teaching, and created a different number of multiple-choice questions as a review. Using the clues and the figure below, determine which Project Manager taught each process, the time required, and the number of review questions.

Note: Knowledge of this chapter in the PMBOK® Guide 2004 is required to do this problem. Also, the names of the people in this problem and the next several problems related to the PMBOK® Guide 2004 are the same, but the first name and last name may not be the same from problem to problem.

Clues:

1. Susan needed two hours to teach the process where the work breakdown structure dictionary was an output and Dirk used nine questions for the process where the work breakdown dictionary (updates) were an output.
2. Alfonso taught one of the modules where expert judgment was a tool and technique.
3. The process where stakeholder analysis was a tool and technique had six test questions, one for each hour of lecture.
4. Maggie used eight test questions and five hours to teach the only process where the scope management plan was not an output.
5. Three hours was required to teach the module where replanning was a tool and technique.
6. The exam with five questions was not with the shortest lecture.

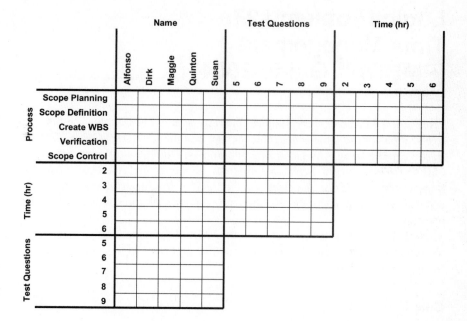

Project Manager	Process	Number of Questions	Time (hr)

Logic Problem #25:
Time Management
(PMBOK® Guide 2004) _____

Five Project Managers were assigned the responsibility of teaching the first five sections of the Time Management chapter in the PMBOK® Guide 2004. Each Project Manager taught a different process, required a different amount of time for teaching, and created a different number of multiple-choice questions as a review. Using the clues and the figure below, determine which Project Manager taught each process, the time required, and the number of review questions.

Note: Knowledge of this chapter in the PMBOK® Guide 2004 is required to do this problem. Consider only the first five processes in this chapter, although there are more.

Clues:

1. The largest number of test questions went with the longest lecture.
2. The process where the WBS dictionary was an input used up all of Dirk's five hours of lecture.
3. The process with the greatest number of tools and techniques was taught in six hours and with only 8 review questions.
4. The process with the least number of outputs was taught by Quinton using 12 test questions, but not in three hours.
5. Maggie used three hours to teach one of the processes where PM software was a tool and technique but did not use 15 test questions.
6. Susan did not teach the process where organizational process assets were an input.

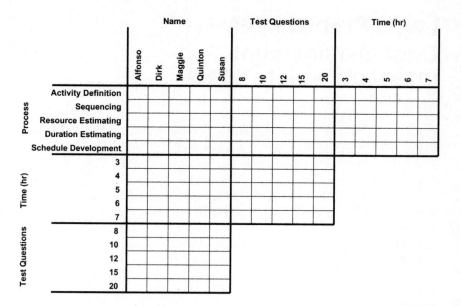

Project Manager	Process	Number of Questions	Time (hr)

Logic Problem #26: Cost Management (PMBOK® Guide 2004) _____

Three Project Managers were assigned the responsibility of teaching the three sections of the Cost Management chapter in the PMBOK® Guide 2004. Each Project Manager taught a different process, required a different amount of time for teaching, and created a different number of multiple-choice questions as a review. Using the clues and the figure below, determine which Project Manager taught each process, the time required, and the number of review questions.

Note: Knowledge of this chapter in the PMBOK® Guide 2004 is required to do this problem.

Clues:

1. Dirk taught the module with the largest number of outputs.
2. Twelve hours was required to teach the module with the largest number of inputs.
3. Nine hours of lectures was used with the only module where PM software was not a tool.
4. Maggie lectured for six hours.

		Name			Test Questions			Time (hr)		
		Alfonso	Dirk	Maggie	10	15	20	6	9	12
Process	Estimating									
	Budgeting									
	Control									
Time (hr)	6									
	9									
	12									
Test Questions	10									
	15									
	20									

Project Manager	Process	Number of Questions	Time (hr)

Logic Problem #27:
Risk Management
(PMBOK® Guide 2004) _____

Five Project Managers were assigned the responsibility of teaching the first five sections of the Risk Management chapter in the PMBOK® Guide 2004. Each Project Manager taught a different process, required a different amount of time for teaching, and created a different number of multiple-choice questions as a review. Using the clues and the figure below, determine which Project Manager taught each process, the time required, and the number of review questions.

Note: Knowledge of this chapter in the PMBOK® Guide 2004 is required to do this problem. Consider only the first five processes in this chapter, although there are more.

Clues:

1. Dirk taught one of the three processes where the risk register (update) was an output but did not use 12 hours or 30 questions.
2. Maggie lectured for 16 hours on the only module with project scope management not an input.
3. Assumption analysis is a tool and technique in the process that requires 8 hours for Susan to teach.
4. Quinton taught one of the two modules where the project management plan is an input; his class did not have 15 questions.
5. The process with the documentation review as a tool had 25 test questions.
6. Alfonso used 15 test questions to go with 10 hours of lectures.
7. The only process with more than one output used 20 questions.

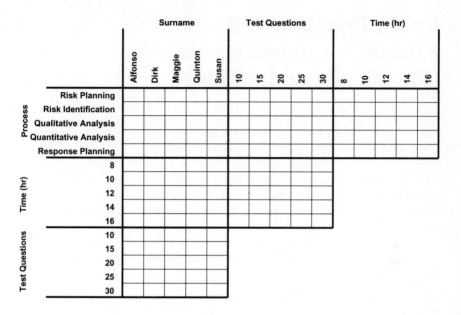

Project Manager	Process	Number of Questions	Time (hr)

Logic Problem #28: Procurement Management (PMBOK® Guide 2004) _____

Five Project Managers were assigned the responsibility of teaching the first five sections of the Procurement Management chapter in the PMBOK® Guide 2004. Each Project Manager taught a different process, required a different amount of time for teaching, and created a different number of multiple-choice questions as a review. Using the clues and the figure below, determine which Project Manager taught each process, the time required, and the number of review questions.

Note: Knowledge of this chapter in the PMBOK® Guide 2004 is required to do this problem. Consider only the first five processes in this chapter, although there are more.

Clues:

1. The make-or-buy analysis required 8 hours of lecture but not by Quinton.
2. The process where the make-or-buy decision is an output required 10 hours of lecture and 30 questions.
3. Dirk discussed bidder conferences in his lectures and 5 of his 25 questions were on this subject.
4. Maggie lectured on the contract evaluation criteria as part of her 6-hour lecture.
5. The 3-hour lecture was not accompanied by 25 test questions; this was not the contract administration process that was covered by Susan's lectures.
6. Vendor payment systems, as a tool and technique, had a 10-question test.
7. The discussion of the contract types, as a tool and technique, as expected had the test with the greatest number of questions.

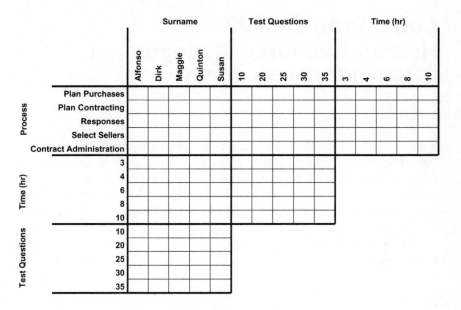

Project Manager	Process	Number of Questions	Time (hr)

Logic Problem #29:
Human Resource Management
(PMBOK® Guide 2004) _____

Four Project Managers were assigned the responsibility of teaching the four sections of the Human Resource Management chapter in the PMBOK® Guide 2004. Each Project Manager taught a different process, required a different amount of time for teaching, and created a different number of multiple-choice questions as a review. Using the clues and the figure below, determine which Project Manager taught each process, the time required, and the number of review questions.

Note: Knowledge of this chapter in the PMBOK® Guide 2004 is required to do this problem.

Clues:

1. Dirk prepared 15 questions for the process with the greatest number of tools and techniques; this process did not involve the least or greatest number of teaching hours.
2. Alfonso spent six hours covering the process where roles and responsibilities were an output.
3. Maggie spent five hours on her module.
4. The module where virtual teams were discussed as tools and techniques had 10 test questions.
5. Quinton used 12 test questions.

			Name				Test Questions				Time (hr)		
		Alfonso	Dirk	Maggie	Quinton	10	12	14	15	3	4	5	6
Process	Human Resource Planning												
	Acquire Team												
	Develop Team												
	Manage Team												
Time (hr)	3												
	4												
	5												
	6												
Test Questions	10												
	12												
	14												
	15												

Project Manager	Process	Number of Questions	Time (hr)

Logic Problem #30: Communications Management (PMBOK® Guide 2004) _____

Four Project Managers were assigned the responsibility of teaching the four sections of the Communications Management chapter in the PMBOK® Guide 2004. Each Project Manager taught a different process, required a different amount of time for teaching, and created a different number of multiple-choice questions as a review. Using the clues and the figure below, determine which Project Manager taught each process, the time required, and the number of review questions.

Note: Knowledge of this chapter in the PMBOK® Guide 2004 is required to do this problem.

Clues:

1. Dirk prepared 10 test questions for the module he was teaching that had a communications management plan as an output; Maggie taught a process area where the communications management plan was an input.

2. The process where lessons learned were part of tools and techniques was taught in 3 hours.

3. Quinton used 2 hours to teach the process area where request changes was an output.

4. Communications methods as tools and techniques had 6 test questions and did not require 5 hours.

5. The 12-question test was in the 3-hour lecture; this was not Alfonso.

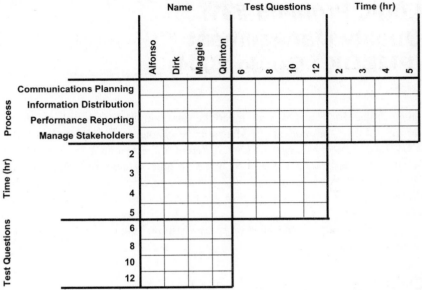

Project Manager	Process	Number of Questions	Time (hr)

Logic Problem #31:
Quality Management
(PMBOK® Guide 2004) _____

Three Project Managers were assigned the responsibility of teaching the three sections of the Communications Management chapter in the PMBOK® Guide 2004. Each Project Manager taught a different process, required a different amount of time for teaching, and created a different number of multiple-choice questions as a review. Using the clues and the figure below, determine which Project Manager taught each process, the time required, and the number of review questions.

Note: Knowledge of this chapter in the PMBOK® Guide 2004 is required to do this problem.

Clues:

1. The place where design of experiments was part of tools and techniques was part of an 8-hour lecture. This was not Maggie.
2. Dirk lectured on Pareto Charts, which was clearly identified under tools and techniques.
3. The output of quality metrics was tested on as part of a 30-question test.
4. Quality audits, as part of tools and techniques, was part of a 10-hour lecture and part of a test that had more than 20 questions.

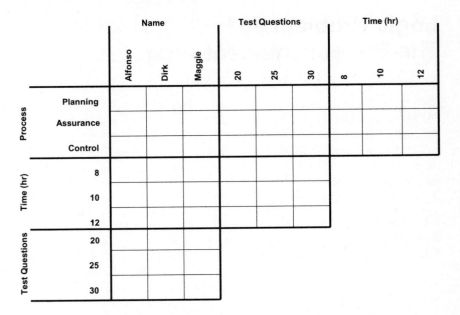

Project Manager	Process	Number of Questions	Time (hr)

Logic Problem #32:
The Project Team Meeting _____

Each week, the Project Manager and the six Assistant Project Managers (APMs) attend a project team meeting. The figure below shows the layout of the conference room where the team meetings are conducted. From the clues below, determine the name and title of each person and their position around the conference table. The Project Manager, as expected, occupies the space at the head of the table.

First Name: Frank; George; Hamilton; Irma; Julie; Kathy; Louise

Surname: Parker; Quade; Roberts; Stippends; Unger; Vixen; Williams

Title: Project Manager; APM Civil Engineering; APM Cost Control; APM Design Engineering; APM Mechanical Engineering; APM Piping Engineering: APM Quality Assurance

Clues:

1. Irma Stippends would like some day to become a Project Manager.
2. George sat between the APM for Cost Control and Unger on one side of the table.
3. Julie sat opposite the APM for Piping Engineering, who had a right-hand neighbor called Williams.
4. The APM for Design Engineering, who is not Frank, was the immediate right-hand neighbor of Hamilton, who did not sit in chair 2 in the conference room.
5. Quade, who was the APM for Mechanical Engineering, sat beside Frank on the same side of the table and opposite Roberts, who did not occupy a middle seat on either long side of the table.

6. The APM for Quality Assurance was sitting in seat 7, immediately to the left of the Project Manager.
7. The Project Manager's first name is Louise, but her surname is not Parker; she was not sitting next to Kathy.

Hint: If you need help, another clue appears on p. 195.

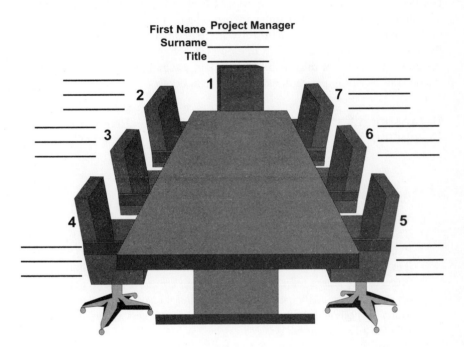
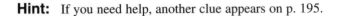

Logic Problem #33:
The PM Software
Exhibitors' Booths _____

Each year, at the annual Project Managers' National Conference, exhibitors are allowed to rent space to display their products. This year, six companies that produce Project Management software rented booths. The six booths for the software exhibitors are shown in the figure below. Using the clues below, determine the name of the company occupying each booth and the name of the person providing the demonstration in each booth.

Representative: Alan; Bill; Ellen; Francine; Gwen; Harry

Company: Bristol Co.; Colgate Co.; Devlin Co.; Egret Co.; Turball Co.; Wallace Co.

Clues:

1. Booth C represents the Devlin Co. software.
2. The Wallace Co. booth is separated from Ellen's booth by the Egret Co. exhibit, which is not on the same side of the aisle as Alan's booth.
3. The two central booths have men performing the demonstrations.
4. None of the letters representing each booth correspond with the first letter in the name of the person demonstrating the software product.
5. Harry's booth is directly opposite Francine's demonstration of the Bristol Co. software products.
6. One of the women demonstrated the Turball Co. software.

Hint: If you need help, another clue appears on p. 195

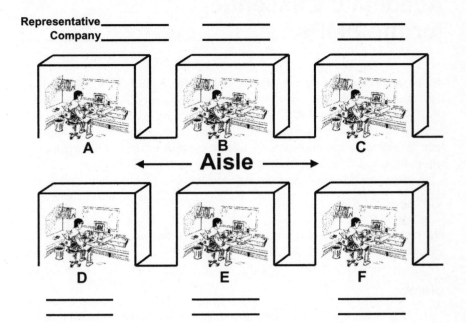

Logic Problem #34: Academic Challenge for the PMPs®

A company decided to hold an academic challenge contest using eight of its newly recognized PMPs®, all of whom had received very high scores on the PMP® exam. The eight PMPs® were assigned at random to two teams, the red team and the blue team, as shown in the figure below. One of the four members of each team was chosen as the team captain. A moderator or quizmaster would then be assigned to challenge each team with questions.

In the figure below, position the eight contestants. Identify their name and the score they received on the PMP® to qualify for the academic challenge.

Name: Alan; Barbara; Christine; David; Elisa; Frank; Gloria; Howard
Score: 190; 191; 192; 193; 194; 195; 196; 197

Clues:

1. Gloria sat between her team captain, who did not receive the highest qualifying score, and the woman who qualified with a score of 191.
2. Frank sat at the furthest point from the quizmaster and next to a woman who scored either 190 or 191; Frank is not on the same team as Howard, who qualified with a score of 196.
3. Christine was sitting opposite David and immediately beside the man who scored 195 to qualify.
4. The total qualifying points for one of the teams was 785 out of a possible 800.
5. Each team consisted of two men and two women, and the person on the team sitting closest to the quizmaster was the team captain.

6. Alan and Elisa, who happened to be one of the qualifiers to score more than 193 on the exam, did not sit side by side and represent the red team.
7. The qualifier who scored 192 points was a woman assigned to the blue team.
8. Barbara was sitting somewhere to the quizmaster's left.

Hint: If you need help, another clue appears on p. 195.

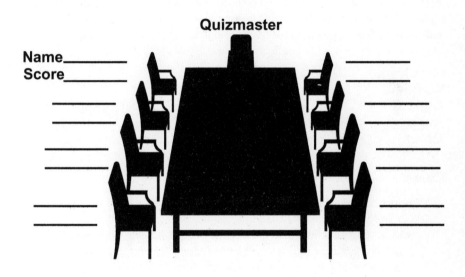

Logic Problem #35: Attending the Safety Briefing _____

A company instituted a new safety program and all of the members of each team were required to attend one of the hourly sessions. Four engineering team members each decided to attend a different briefing session. Using the figure below and the clues, determine the name of each member, their title, and the time they showed up for the briefing.

First Name: Alfred; Bob; Carl; David
Surname: Edwards; Franklin; Graham; Hill
Title: Civil Engineer; Electrical Engineer; Manufacturing Engineer; Mechanical Engineer
Time: 1:00 p.m.; 2:00 p.m.; 3:00 p.m.; 4:00 p.m.

Clues:

1. Edwards is the Manufacturing Engineer.
2. Carl and Franklin share the same office.
3. Alfred felt that it was unnecessary for his Mechanical Engineering group to hear the briefing, but he went along anyway.
4. David attended the session immediately after Graham's session but immediately before the session attended by the Civil Engineer.
5. The Electrical Engineer, who happens to play golf with Bob, attended the 4:00 p.m. briefing session, which was the last session for the day.

First Name_____

Surname_____

Title_____

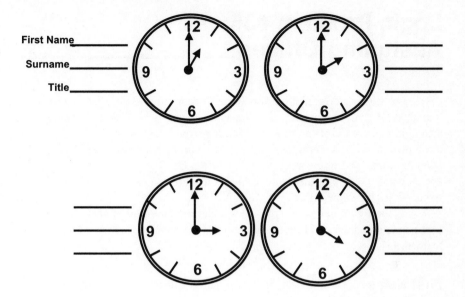

Logic Problem #36:
Assigning Offices _____

Office space was a critical issue for Acme Corporation because its customers indicated a strong preference for collocated teams. Five offices were made available in a corner of the building. Ten team members were to be assigned to these offices, with two employees per office. On the team were two employees from Accounting, Engineering, Manufacturing, Quality, and Scheduling. The decision was made that the two employees from the same functional group would share the same office.

Using the figure below and the clues, determine the title of each office; the first name, surname, and title of each employee; and the office in which they resided.

First Name: Andrew; Barry; Cedric; Dora; Eileen; Frank; Gertrude; Henrietta; Iggy; Joseph

Surname: Maxwell; Newman; Oregon; Pringle; Quiggly; Richardson; Stone;Turner; Wilson; Vargo

Office: Accounting; Engineering; Manufacturing; Quality; Scheduling

Clues:

1. Eileen Newman works in the office across from Accounting, where Frank and Quiggly reside.
2. Stone's first name is not Henrietta and the person that shares the latter's office is not Oregon.
3. Iggy, who is not Maxwell, works in the office bordered on one side by Barry Wilson's office, which is not office 5, and the Quality office.
4. Dora, who works in an office opposite to Maxwell, is not in an office opposite or adjacent to Engineering.
5. Office 4 is the Scheduling office. Joseph, who previously never worked on any project teams with Turner, and Vargo reside in the Scheduling office.

6. Pringle and Richardson share the same office; the first name of the former alphabetically precedes his officemate.
7. Andrew and Cedric share an office.
8. The Manufacturing office, where Stone resides, and the Engineering office are side by side on one side of the aisle.

Hint: If you need help, another clue appears on p. 195.

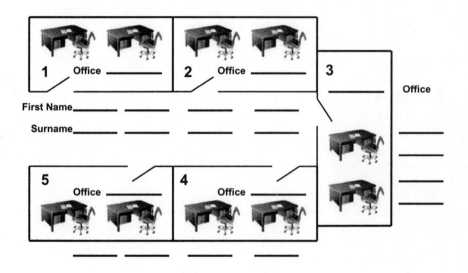

Logic Problem #37: Positioning the Quality Awards _____

A company received eight quality awards for excellence in some area of quality. Each award came from a different customer. The awards were hung on a wall, as shown in the figure below. Using the clues, determine the company from which the award was received and the reason for the award.

Company: Argotech; Botson; Chilling; Ducor; Edgewood; Mowtex; Wilson; Zeno

Reason for Award: On-Time Delivery; Low-Cost Production; Product Quality; Product Design; Superior Overall Performance; Ten Years of Partnership Excellence; Breakthrough in Technology; Customer Support

Clues:

1. The top row contains the awards received from Ducor and Edgewood.
2. Chilling did not provide the Product Quality Award and the position of the Chilling award is not immediately below the Edgewood award.
3. The Wilson award for a breakthrough in technology is immediately below the award recognizing product design.
4. The award recognizing superior overall performance is immediately above the award recognizing 10 years of partnership excellence.

5. The Argotech award is positioned between the Zeno award for customer support, which is not on either end of a row, and the award for low-cost production.
6. The award for on-time delivery is in position 8 while the Botson award is at the other extreme end of the same row.

Hint: If you need help, another clue appears on p. 195.

1
Company_____   2 _____   3_____   4_____
Reason_____   _____   _____   _____

5_____   6_____   7_____   8_____
_____   _____   _____   _____

Logic Problem #38: Recognition for Safety Adherence _____

Once every three months, the company selects six people that have demonstrated outstanding recognition for adherence to safety requirements. Each of the six people pick a gift box in which are gifts or certificates for gifts. In the figure below are the six gift boxes. Using the clues provided, determine which box each person selected and the award they received.

Name: John; Betty; Carol; Dora; Steven; Wade
Award: $1500; $1000; Management Granted Time Off; Stereo; Gift Certificate; Use of the Company Car

Clues:

1. Wade's award, which was not in the form of cash, was in a box in the row above the box with the gift for use of the company car.
2. The larger of the two cash awards was in gift box 1, but unfortunately Dora selected a different numbered box.
3. The smaller cash award was in a box to the left of the box that Betty chose.
4. Carol selected her favorite number, 6, which was not the Management Granted Time Off Award.
5. John received the gift certificate; his gift was located to the right of the box containing the stereo as a gift.

Hint: If you need help, another clue appears on p. 195.

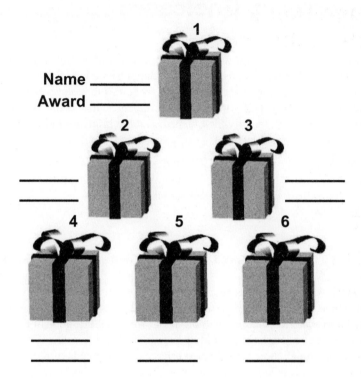

Logic Problem #39:
The Company Briefcases _____

A company provides use of special company briefcases to its employees when the employees are traveling to customers to make presentations. In the same week, five Project Managers were traveling to five cities to make presentations to their customers. Using the figure below and the clues, determine the name of each Project Manager, the city they visited, and the briefcase they selected.

First Name: Evelyn; Florence; Gerald; Mark; Richard
Surname: Davis; Greenwood; Hampton; Norwell; Powell
City: Boston; Chicago; Denver; Miami; Phoenix

Clues:

1. Mark Hampton was delighted to just get out of the office for a few days and travel.
2. Norwell selected the briefcase in position 1.
3. Davis was unsure as to which city he would be flying to for his presentation because his customer had offices in Miami, Chicago, and Denver.
4. Florence had a tough time deciding which briefcase to select. She narrowed down her choices to the two briefcases at the ends of the row.
5. Greenwood's briefcase selection for a trip to Miami stands next to Richard's choice, which is not in an even-numbered position.

6. Gerald looked forward to his trip to Boston; his briefcase selection is further to the left than Evelyn's selection.
7. The briefcase in position 4 was carried to Denver.

Hint: If you need help, another clue appears on p. 195.

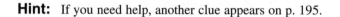

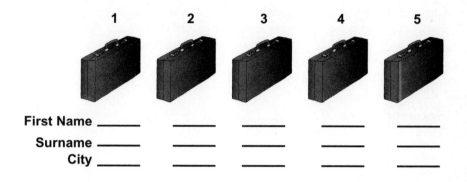

First Name _____   _____   _____   _____   _____
Surname _____   _____   _____   _____   _____
City _____   _____   _____   _____   _____

Logic Problem #40:
Offices for the
Project Sponsors _____

The president of a company decided that the six executives that were functioning as executive project sponsors should be located on the same floor on the building. On this floor, there just happened to be six large offices, as shown in the figure below. Using the clues below, determine the name, title, and office for each of the executive sponsors.

Sponsor: Hendrix; Jackson; Mulligan; Nixon; Pullman; Sommerville
Title: VP Information Technology; VP Engineering; VP R&D; VP Manufacturing; VP Quality; VP Marketing

Clues:

1. Office 2 is Hendrix.
2. Office 4 is the VP for Marketing
3. Mulligan and the VP for Quality have adjacent offices but on different sides of the hallway.
4. Jackson's office is numbered two higher than the VP for R&D.
5. Nixon, the VP for Engineering, has an office numbered two higher than Mulligan's office and immediately across the hall from the VP for Information Technology, whose surname has more letters than the VP for R&D.

Hint: If you need help, another clue appears on p. 195.

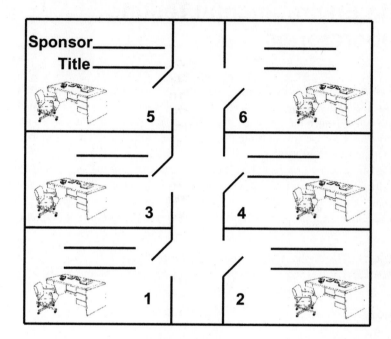

Logic Problem #41:
The Environmental Testing
Laboratories _____

The company has a policy that, before final project closure, all products from
the projects must undergo environmental protection testing. Testing usually requires about four hours. The test facility has five small laboratories so that
testing can be done for multiple projects at the same time. The figure below
shows the five laboratories.

On one day, five projects had their products tested at the same time. Using
the clues below, determine which projects were in which laboratories and the
amount of time remaining for the testing. One project was completely tested,
and the other four projects had different time remaining before completion.

Project: Alpha; Beta; Gamma; Delta; Epsilon
Time Left: Testing completed; 1 hour; 1.5 hours; 2 hours; 2.5 hours

Clues:

1. There was one hour remaining on the testing in laboratory 1.
2. Laboratory 5 had more time remaining in its testing than the Epsilon
   Project.
3. The Delta Project was being tested in the laboratory immediately to the
   left of the laboratory that had just finished its testing.

4. The Epsilon Project testing was being conducted in the laboratory immediately to the right of the laboratory with two hours remaining on the testing.
5. The Beta Project was not in the laboratory immediately to the left of the laboratory that finished testing.

Hint: If you need help, another clue appears on p. 195.

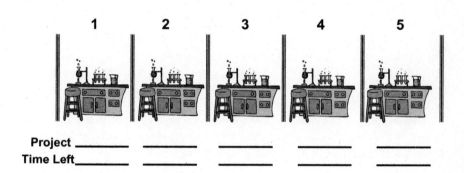

Project _____ _____ _____ _____ _____
Time Left_____ _____ _____ _____ _____

Logic Problem #42:
The Bidders' Conference _____

Seventeen companies had bid on a lucrative government contract. After the announcement of the winning bidder for the contract award, the remaining 16 bidders were invited to a bidders' conference so that the government could explain why their bids were downgraded.

Each bidder submitted a proposal made up of four volumes: Project Management Skills; Technical Approach; Cost; and Previous Performance on government contracts. Each volume was evaluated on points against a specific criterion and, if the criterion was not met, points were taken off. Each bidder was significantly downgraded on only one of the four volumes, but the downgrading was sufficient such that they did not win the contract.

The 16 companies that did not win the contract were seated in the 16 seats shown in the figure below. Using the figure and the clues, determine who sat in each seat and the volume of their proposal that was downgraded.

Name: Carol; Charles; David; Frank; Gilda; Gus; Kathy; Lori; Louis; Paul; Paula; Phil; Rachael; Richard; Steve; Victor

Volume: Project Management; Cost; Past Performance; Technical Approach

Clues:

1. Each row and column in the seating contained each of four volumes that were downgraded.
2. Frank, who was sitting in either the first or second column but not in the second row, was sitting immediately in front of Gilda and immediately behind Paul, who was not sitting in the first row.
3. Louis was sitting is seat 12; Richard was sitting in seat 13 and in the same diagonal line as Rachael, who was sitting in the same row as Phil.
4. David was sitting between Gilda and Paula in the same row.
5. Gus was the only male in the room that represented a company that was downgraded because of poor project management skills.
6. Charles, who was sitting in the same column as Paul, had Kathy sitting to his immediate right as you look at the figure.

7. Steve, Rachael, and another woman represented companies that had their Cost volume downgraded.
8. Victor and Gus sat in the first row with Gus occupying a lower numbered seat.
9. Carol was sitting in the row above Lori and diagonally to her left as you look at the figure.
10. Four men in the bidders' conference represented the four companies that had their Past Performance volume downgraded.

Hint: If you need help, another clue appears on p. 195.

Name

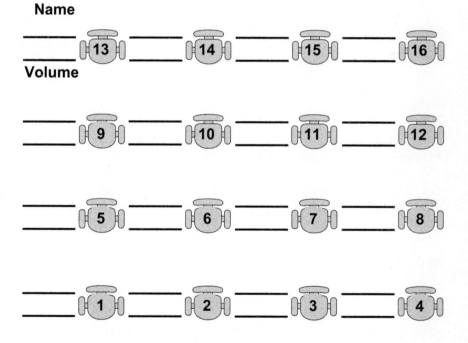

Volume

Logic Problem #43:
The Train Ride to Work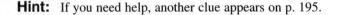

Alpha Company is located in the center of town. Five of the employees of Alpha Company commute to work each day by taking a train to work. The five employees are all working on the same project and sit together on the train discussing the daily problems on the project. The names and titles of the people are shown below together with a figure identifying the stops where the five employees board the train. Using the clues below, identify the name and title of each employee and the stop where they board the train.

Name: Alex; Barbara; Carla; Edward; Paul
Title: Cost Accountant; Design Engineer; Project Manager; Procurement Specialist; Quality Assurance Specialist

Clues:

1. Carla boards the train immediately before the Cost Accountant.
2. Barbara, who has never functioned as a Project Manager, boards the train immediately before Paul.
3. The Project Manager boards the train immediately after Edward.
4. Alex has a longer train ride than the Quality Assurance Specialist.
5. The Design Engineer is one stop closer to work (according to the figure) than the Procurement Specialist.

Hint: If you need help, another clue appears on p. 195.

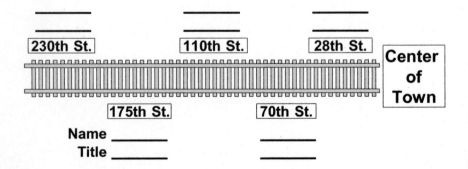

Logic Problem #44:
Customer Shipping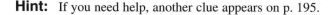

A company mass produces certain products for its customers. Each customer is viewed as a project and a Project Manager is assigned to each customer. Once the products are manufactured, they are packaged and stored on the shipping dock awaiting shipping.

In the figure below are five packages waiting for shipment. Using the clues, identify the name of each Project Manager, his or her customer's name, and the number of units in the package.

PM: Bosworth; McGill; Neville; Prince; Reynolds
Customer: Apex; Convex; Dixon; Quartz; Yarmouth
Units: 100; 200; 350; 600; 800

Clues:

1. The package with 350 units will be shipped to Quartz Corporation; this package is positioned more than one space to the right of the package with 600 units.
2. McGill is not the Project Manager for the package in position 1.
3. The package with 200 units is immediately to the left of Bosworth's package but immediately to the right of the package going to Apex Corporation.
4. The package that Prince worked on is immediately to the right of Neville's package and immediately to the left of the package with 800 units, which is immediately to the left of the package being shipped to Dixon.
5. The package being shipped to Convex Industries is immediately to the left of the package in which Reynolds was the Project Manager; the latter has 200 more units than the former.

Hint: If you need help, another clue appears on p. 195.

PM _____ _____ _____ _____ _____
Customer _____ _____ _____ _____ _____
Units _____ _____ _____ _____ _____

Logic Problem #45:
The Luncheon Meeting _____

Four Project Managers always eat lunch together in the company cafeteria.
During lunch, the Project Managers complained about the cost overruns they
were experiencing on their projects. Each Project Manager had a different size
cost overrun and each overrun was for a different reason. Using the figure below and the clues, determine the position of each Project Manager, the reason
for their cost overrun, and the size of the cost overrun.

Name: Maxine; Jerry; Ned; Sandra
Reason: Bad Weather; Wrong Materials; Inexperienced Workers;
            Equipment Breakdown
Size: $40K; $50K; $60K; $70K

Clues:

1. Jerry's cost overrun was $50K.
2. Sandra was not sitting in chair 2 in the figure.
3. Wrong material accounted for the smallest cost overrun.
4. Bad weather was the reason given for the cost overrun by the person
   sitting in chair 1.
5. Maxine's cost overrun was because of inexperienced workers; her
   overrun was less than the cost incurred because of the equipment
   breakdown.
6. Ned was sitting in the next seat clockwise from the Project Manager
   that was discussing the breakdown in equipment.

Hint: If you need help, another clue appears on p. 195.

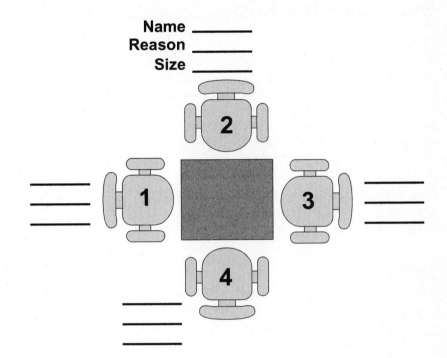

Logic Problem #46:
Security Check-In _____

Because of security reasons, all employees are given security badges that must be inserted into a scanner as the employees enter the building. There is only one scanner, and all employees must form a single line.

Four Project Managers stood in line together waiting to enter the building. Each Project Manager worked on a different floor in the building. Using the clues and the figure below, determine the full name of each Project Manager, the floor they work on, and their position in line.

First Name: Andrea; Becky; Charlene; Denise
Surname: Fiorella; Glass; Hendrix; Imwell
Floor: 1; 2; 3; 4

Clues:

1. Andrea immediately precedes Imwell in the line.
2. The person who works on the second floor immediately precedes Becky in line.
3. The first person in line, which is not Charlene, works on the third floor.
4. Denise, who works on the fourth floor, is not Glass and is not in position 2 in line.
5. The Project Manager named Hendrix works on the first floor.

Hint: If you need help, another clue appears on p. 195.

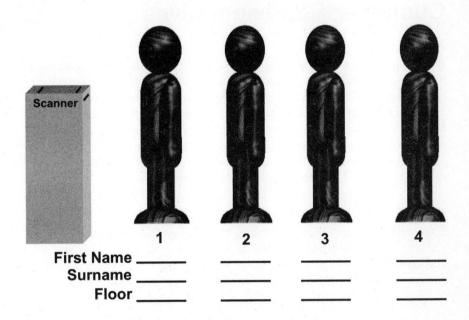

Logic Problem #47: Customer Representatives _____

As part of the contractual terms and conditions, the customer has demanded that four customer representatives be located in your building for the duration of the project. Representatives are to have their own offices. Each representative has a different area of expertise and each has a different amount of experience. Your company found a small alcove in the building and has assigned offices 405–408 to the customer's onsite representatives.

Using the figure below and the clues, determine the name of the person in each office, their area of expertise, and the number of years of experience.

Name: George; Hilda; Rex; Susan

Expertise: Engineering; Quality; Manufacturing; Earned Value Measurement (EVM)

Experience: 15 years; 20 years, 22 years, 25 years

Clues:

1. The man in office 408 is not responsible for Engineering, and the person with 22 years of experience was not assigned to office 405.
2. The person with the Manufacturing expertise has the fewest years of experience among the four representatives.
3. Susan has a great deal of expertise in Quality.
4. The person with Earned Value Measurement expertise has an office located between the office where Rex, the person with the greatest number of years of experience, is located and the main corridor.

Hint: If you need help, another clue can be found on p. 196.

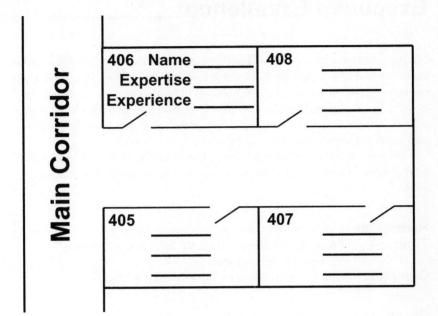

Logic Problem #48:
Executive Excellence _____

For the past four years, the local PMI® chapter presented a yearly award to an executive from the local community that has demonstrated excellence in project management either by functioning as an executive sponsor or support in general for project management, including support for the local PMI® chapter. At this year's award banquet, the pictures of the recipients from the previous four years are hung on the Wall of Honor.

Using the figure below and the clues, determine the name of the person who won the award in each year, their title, and the company for which they work.

Name: Merriman; Richardson; Stevenson; Wilson
Title: President; VP Engineering; VP Information Systems;
                 VP Project Management
Company: Alcax Corp.; Boomer Corp.; Condiphor Co.; Dalpro, Inc.

Clues:

1. Richardson is an officer with Condiphor Company.
2. The Vice President for Engineering is an officer with Alcax Corporation.
3. The 2003 award winner was an officer who functioned as the Vice President for Project Management.

4. Merriman was the winner of the award in 2004; however, the award winner for the next year did not come from Dalpro, Inc.
5. The award winner from Boomer Corporation is positioned next to Stevenson, the only award winner who was not a Vice President.

Hint: If you need help, another clue can be found on p. 196.

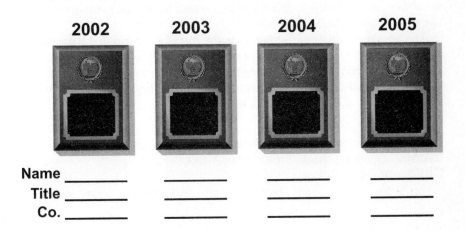

2002   **2003**   **2004**   **2005**

Name _____   _____   _____   _____
Title _____   _____   _____   _____
Co. _____   _____   _____   _____

Logic Problem #49: Project Team Housing _____

Your company has just won a large contract with a foreign client. The project requires that five of your team members be relocated to the client's country for at least one year. The client has graciously agreed to provide housing for the five team members and their families.

The housing consists of five homes at the end of a street called Rainbow Alley. Each home is a different color and each family residing in the home has a different number of children. Using the figure below and the clues, determine the name of the family that lives in each home, the color of the home, and the number of children in the family.

Family: Adams; Berger; Chalmers; Davidson; Edgewater
Color: Gray; Black; Brown; Blue; White
Children: 0; 1; 2; 3; 4

Clues:

1. House 123 has no children.
2. House 124 is not painted gray.
3. The Berger family of three live immediately opposite the house painted brown.
4. House 121 is painted white.
5. The Chalmers family live in a blue house.

6. The Adams family lives in house 122 but do not have four children.
7. The house painted black has a family with two children; this is not house 125 on Rainbow Alley. However, it is on the opposite side of Rainbow Alley from where the Edgewater family lives, but not directly opposite.

Hint: If you need help, another clue appears on p. 196.

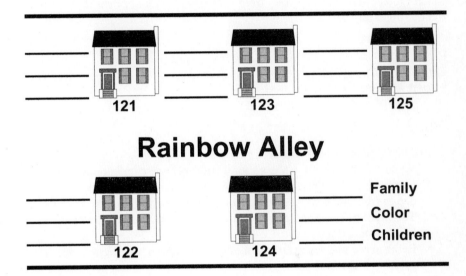

Rainbow Alley

Family
Color
Children

Logic Problem #50:
Flying to the Customer _____

Four Project Managers were flying to different cities to meet with their customers. As it happened, they were all flying the same airline and departing from the same concourse. Using the figure below and the clues, determine which Project Managers departed from each gate, the city of their destination, and the flight number.

PM: Anderson; Bellman; Wellington; Wylie
City: Chicago; Denver; Detroit; Los Angeles
Flight #: 581; 604; 1023; 2044

Clues:

1. The flight to Detroit was departing from gate 31.
2. Wylie was heading to Chicago for a customer presentation meeting.
3. Flight 581, which was not Anderson's flight number, was scheduled to depart from the next gate anticlockwise from the flight going to Denver.
4. The flight to Los Angeles is directly across from flight 604, which was Wellington's flight.
5. Bellman did not depart from either gate 28, which was flight 2044, or gate 29, which was not flight 1023.

Hint: If you need help, another clue appears on p. 196.

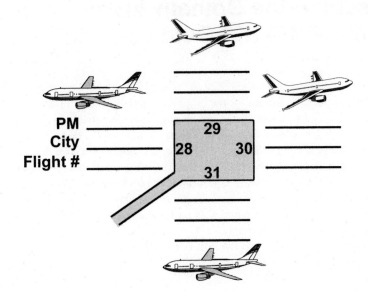

PM _____

City _____

Flight # _____

Logic Problem #51:
Teaching the Domain Areas of the PMBOK® Guide _____

When the 2004 version of the PMBOK® Guide came out, a company decided to set up a training program for the employees to become familiar with the changes. The decision was made that all employees involved in projects must attend a one-hour session on each of the six domain areas. Because of employee work loads and schedules, all six domain areas would be taught on Monday, Tuesday, and Wednesday of the following week, but in different time slots each day. For example, if Initiation were taught on Monday in the first session, it could not be taught on Tuesday or Wednesday in the same first session of the day. Employees could sign up for the training on Initiation for Monday, Tuesday, or Wednesday.

Using the clues below and the figure, determine in which time slots each domain area was taught each day.

Domain Area: Initiation; Planning; Execution; Control; Closure; Professional Responsibility

Clues:

1. On Tuesday, Planning is not taught in the middle of the afternoon; on the same day, training on Initiation immediately follows the training session on Closure.
2. Monday's training session on the Control domain area is taught in the same session in the morning as Wednesday's afternoon session.
3. Session 3 on Monday afternoon, session 1 on Tuesday afternoon, and Wednesday's session 2 in the morning all have the same domain area being taught.
4. Initiation is taught immediately following Closure without a lunch break on Wednesday, though it is not session 3 in the morning.
5. Session 1 on Wednesday morning covers the Planning domain area.
6. Monday's session on Planning immediately follows the session on Execution, with or without a break for lunch.

7. Monday's first session in the afternoon is the Closure domain area.
8. Tuesday's session on the Control domain area, which is not session 2 in either the morning or afternoon, takes place at the same time of day as Wednesday's session covering the Execution domain area.

Hint: If you need help, another clue appears on p. 196.

Morning	Monday	Tuesday	Wednesday
Session 1			
Session 2			
Session 3			
Afternoon	Lunch		
Session 1			
Session 2			
Session 3			

Logic Problem #52: Capacity Planning _____

As business began to expand, Acme Corporation realized that it needed additional warehouse capacity. Four warehouses were built in four towns. A map is shown below. Each warehouse was painted a different color and had a different capacity. Using the figure below and the clues, determine the location of each town on the map, the color of the warehouse, and the capacity of each warehouse.

Town: Bell; Collins; Heppy; Wells
Color: Red; White; Black; Green
Capacity: 80,000; 160,000; 280,000; 400,000 (all in square feet)

Clues:

1. The white warehouse is due west from the intersection of the roads.
2. The warehouse with the greatest capacity is not painted black.
3. The warehouse in the due-south position from the intersection of the roads will take you to the town called Wells; this warehouse does not have a capacity of 160,000 square feet.
4. The warehouse in Heppy is in the opposite direction to the green warehouse that has a capacity of 280,000 square feet.
5. The red warehouse in Collins is not as large as the warehouse in Bell and cannot be reached by proceeding east.

Hint: If you need help, another clue appears on p. 196.

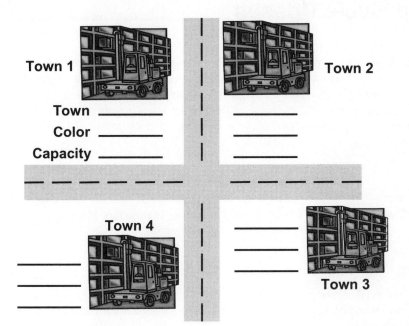

Town 1

Town _____
Color _____
Capacity _____

Town 2

_____
_____
_____

Town 4

_____
_____
_____

_____
_____
_____

Town 3

Logic Problem #53:
Life-Cycle Phases _____

On the desk of the project sponsor were four reports, each one from a different
information systems project and each project in a different life-cycle phase.
From the clues provided below and the figure, determine which report was in
each position on the desk, the name of the Project Manager who prepared the
report, the life-cycle phase discussed in the report, and the nature of each
project.

PM: Agnes; Bobbi; Ethel; Thomas
Project: Estimating; Salary Deductions; Benefits; Shipping
Life-Cycle Phase: Requirements Definition; Preliminary Planning;
Detailed Planning; Execution

Clues:

1. The project managed by Thomas covers the completion of the preliminary planning life-cycle phase, but his project does not involve salary
   deductions.
2. The report in position 4 does not discuss the completion of the requirements definition life-cycle phase.

3. The report discussing the shipping project, which was prepared by the Project Manager called Bobbi, is one position to the right of the report covering the completion of the execution phase of a project.
4. The report on the estimating project covers the detailed planning life-cycle phase.
5. Ethel's report is in position 3 on the desk.

Hint: If you need help, another clue is provided on p. 196.

```
           PM _____    _____   _____   _____
      Project _____    _____   _____   _____
Life-Cycle Phase _____    _____   _____   _____
```

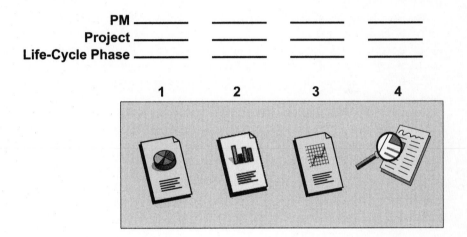

Logic Problem #54:
Reporting Gifts Received _____

A Project Manager just returned from a visit to the country of Dravonia where the Project Manager made a presentation to several senior government officials concerning the successful completion of the project. One of the traditions in Dravonia is to provide the Project Manager with gifts if the project is completed successfully.

Knowing that receiving gifts may be a violation of Professional Responsibility for Project Managers and possibly a violation of the Code of Professional Conduct, the Project Manager decided to declare all gifts received to the legal department in his company. Each gift was different and had a different cash value assigned to it. Each gift was also received from a different minister in Dravonia.

Using the figure below and the clues, determine the position of each gift, the value of each gift, the nature of each gift, and from which minister the gift was received.

Gift: Coat; Vase; Picture; Statue
Minister: Education; Finance; Trade; Economic Development
Value: $200; $300; $600; $1000

Clues:

1. The $1000 picture, which is not in position 4, was not received from the Minister for Economic Development.
2. The lowest valued gift came from the Minister of Finance.

3. The gift in position 1 was valued at $600.
4. The coat, which was a gift from the Minister of Trade, is positioned immediately to the left of the $300 gift, which was not the vase.

Hint: If you need help, another hint appears on p. 196.

Logic Problem #55:
Taking Vacation _____

It was time to plan for the family vacation. Five Project Managers, each having accrued a different amount of vacation time, decided to take their vaca-
tions in different months. Using the clues below and the figure, determine the
full name of each Project Manager, how much vacation time they had planned
to take, and the month in which the vacation would be taken.

Clues:

1. All of the vacation days are taken in one month.
2. Fleetwater planned on taking her 12 days of vacation in a month later
   than Frank's vacation month.
3. Dennis took his 10 days of vacation in the month following Anderson
   but two months ahead of Vanessa.
4. Andrew's vacation was in September, and Stephanovic preferred June.
5. Burrows had been with the company the shortest amount of time and
   had only 5 days of vacation available.
6. One of the men took an 8-day vacation in July.

	Surname					Days of Vacation					Month				
	Anderson	Burrows	Clearington	Fleetwater	Stephanovic	5	8	10	12	15	May	June	July	August	September
Andrew															
Bridget															
Dennis															
Frank															
Vanessa															
May															
June															
July															
August															
September															
5															
8															
10															
12															
15															

First Name	Surname	Vacation Days	Month

Logic Problem #56:
Meeting with the Customer _____

Five Project Managers were requested by their customers to travel to their customers for an important meeting. Using the clues below and the figure, determine the full name of each Project Manager, their departure day of the week, and the day they returned.

Clues:

1. Anthony Franklin departed on a Wednesday and returned some time the same week.
2. The person who departed on a Friday for a weekend meeting with the customer returned the following Monday. This was the only Project Manager that was gone over the weekend.
3. Denise and Natalie Ashcroft were the only two people fortunate to have their clients in town; they departed and returned the same day.
4. Carlton, who is not Barry, was gone from work three full days in the same week and missed his Tuesday afternoon golf game.
5. Bellows returned to work on Tuesday.
6. Richardson did not depart for his meeting on a Thursday.

		Surname					Depart					Return				
		Ashcroft	Bellows	Carlton	Franklin	Richardson	Monday	Tuesday	Wednesday	Thursday	Friday	Monday	Tuesday	Wednesday	Thursday	Friday
First Name	Anthony															
	Barry															
	Denise															
	Larry															
	Natalie															
Return	Monday															
	Tuesday															
	Wednesday															
	Thursday															
	Friday															
Depart	Monday															
	Tuesday															
	Wednesday															
	Thursday															
	Friday															

First Name	Surname	Departure	Return

Logic Problem #57:
Report Writing _____

Four Project Managers had a meeting with their executive sponsor and were discussing the type of Earned Value Management report they enjoyed preparing themselves rather than delegating the tasks to the team. Using the figure below and the clues, determine the first and last name of the Project Manager in each position and their preference for preparing parts of the Earned Value Management reports.

First Name: Herbert; Jason; Kerrie; Linda
Surname: Pancoe; Bliss; Smith; Walters
Report Type: Progress; Status; Forecast; Exception

Clue:

1. Herbert's surname is not Bliss.
2. As you look at the figure, Smith is positioned immediately to the right of the person who preferred preparing the Status Report who is not Kerrie or Linda.
3. The person in position 2 likes to prepare the Forecast Report.
4. Kerrie Pancoe is not the one who prefers preparing the Progress Report.
5. Walters prefers preparing the Exception Report but the first name is not Linda.

Hint: If you need help, another clue appears on p. 196.

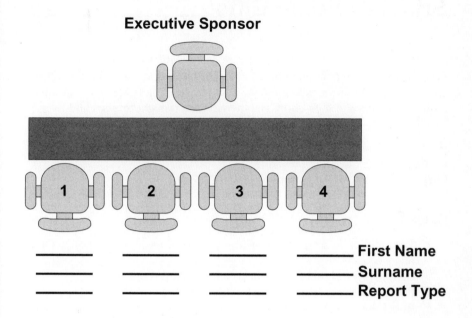

Executive Sponsor

First Name
Surname
Report Type

Logic Problem #58:
Bringing Home Gifts _____

Four Project Managers just returned home from visits to their foreign clients. Each Project Manager brought home a gift for his or her child. Using the figure below and the clues, determine the name of the Project Manager in each position, the name of their child, and the gift they brought for the child.

PM: Alice; Paul; Victor; Zoe
Child: Bobbi; Charlie; Megan; Tommy
Gift: Clothes; Toys; Pictures; Foreign Currency

Clues:

1. The child of the Project Manager in position 3 received the foreign currency coins.
2. Charlie is the child of the Project Manager in position 4.
3. Paul is not the Project Manager in position 2.
4. Bobbi, who received the toys, is seated in a higher position in the figure than Victor's child.
5. Tommy is not the child that received the pictures.
6. Alice's child liked the clothes as gifts.

Hint: If you need help, another clue appears on p. 196.

	1	2	3	4
PM	———	———	———	———
Child	———	———	———	———
Gift	———	———	———	———

Logic Problem #59: Positioning the Team _____

In the figure below, the Project Manager is conducting a team meeting with his eight team members, four men and four women. Using the clues, determine the first name, surname, and position of the eight team members.

First Name: Adam; George; Harriet; Jordan; Rebecca; Sue; Theresa, Victor

Surname: Carlton; Franklin; Gregory; Harwood; Michaels; Newell; Peck; Rim

Clues:

1. Rebecca Newell is sitting in an odd-numbered seat.
2. Theresa, who is not the woman with a surname of Peck, is in seat 5.
3. Franklin sits in seat 1.
4. Harriet is sitting immediately to the right of Jordan as they face the center of the table.
5. Sue and George sit on the same side of the table.
6. Carlton and Rim also sit on the same side of the table with Rim sitting in a higher numbered seat.
7. There are two men and two women on each side of the table; none of the men sit side by side but two of the women sit side by side.
8. Victor sits immediately across from Gregory but not at either end of the table.
9. Harwood has a female team member on either side.

Hint: If you need help, another clue appears on p. 196.

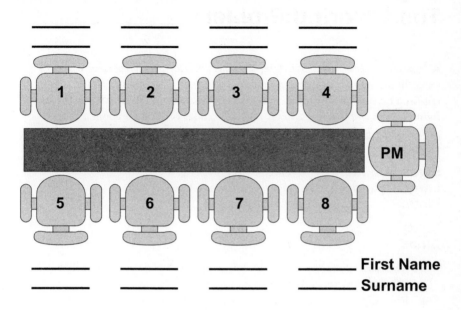

First Name
Surname

Logic Problem #60:
The Coloring Problem _____

A customer placed a special order for four products. Each product had a metallic plate and two cylinders as shown in the figure below. The customer required that all of the cylinders and plates be colored differently. Using the figure below and the clues, determine the colors of each component in each position.

Small Cylinder: Red; Orange; Yellow; Green
Large Cylinder: Blue; Purple; Brown; Black
Plate: Maroon; Olive; Beige; Gray

Clues:

1. The black cylinder was to the left of the gray plate and the yellow cylinder was positioned further to the right than both of them.
2. The beige plate was positioned between the brown cylinder on the left and the red cylinder on the right.
3. The red cylinder and the blue cylinder were not part of the same product, nor were the green and brown components.
4. The purple cylinder was immediately to the left of the olive component; the green component was further left than both of these.

Hint: If you need help, another clue appears on p. 196.

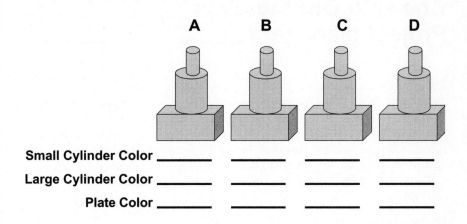

Small Cylinder Color _____   _____   _____   _____

Large Cylinder Color _____   _____   _____   _____

Plate Color _____   _____   _____   _____

Logic Problem #61: Chewing Out the Project Managers _____

The president of the company was briefed on the performance to date of all of the projects under way. Four of the projects were in serious trouble. The president decided to reprimand these four Project Managers and express his concern about the importance of these four projects. The figure shows the four Project Managers and the president. Using the figure and the clues below, identify the name of each Project Manager, the reason for their problem, and the cost overrun that the president appeared worried about.

Name: Barbara; Clarissa; Fred; George
Problem: Poor Quality: Design Flaws; Cost Escalations; Poor Coding
Overrun: $30K; $50K; $60K; $80K

Clues:

1. George was sitting in seat 4.
2. Barbara was reprimanded about the problem with coding earlier than the person in seat 3.
3. The president reprimanded the Project Managers in order of size of their cost overruns beginning with the smallest cost overrun first.
4. The problem with cost escalations was the headache of the person in seat 1.
5. The flaws in the design of one product resulted in a $30K overrun thus far.
6. Fred was not the last person to be reprimanded.
7. Clarissa's problem had nothing to do with quality.

Hint: If you need help, another clue appears on p. 196.

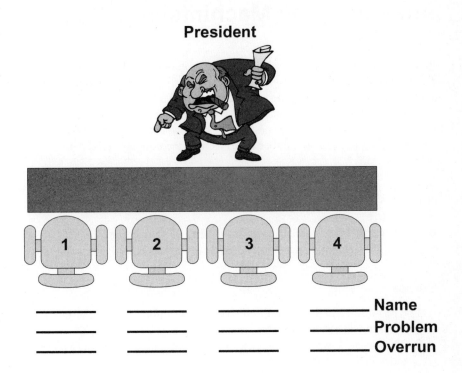

President

Logic Problem #62: Assigning the Machinists _____

Four machinists have their workstations along an aisle in the machine shop. The positions of the machinists are shown in the figure below. Each machinist happens to be a different grade level ranging from a Grade 5 to a Grade 8. Each had been working as a machinist with the company for a different number of years. Using the figure and the clues below, determine the name of each machinist, the pay grade, number of years with the company, and their position.

Name: Bryan; Carl; Edward; Horace
Pay Grade: 5; 6; 7; 8
Experience: 10 years; 12 years; 14 years; 18 years (Note: years of experience and pay grade do not necessarily correspond.)

Clues:

1. The Grade 5 is positioned in the first workstation as you enter the hallway; this is not Horace.
2. The Grade 7, who has 14 years of experience, is not Edward, who resides in workstation 4.
3. Carl and the Grade 10 are on the same side of the aisle.
4. The Grade 8 has a lower numbered workstation than the person with 18 years of experience.
5. The person with 12 years of experience, who is not the Grade 6, occupies workstation 3.

Hint: If you need help, another clue appears on p. 196.

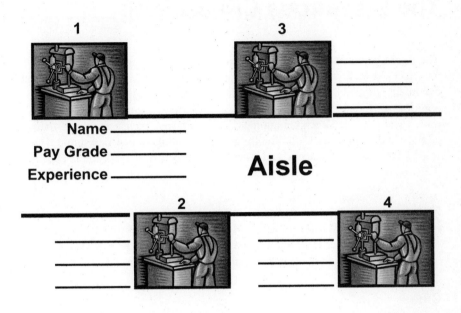

Name —————
Pay Grade —————
Experience —————

Aisle

Logic Problem #63:
The Disastrous Critical Path _____

The figure below shows the seven activities that comprised the critical path of a project. As luck would have it, each of the seven activities had problems and eventually slipped to the point where the project's critical path was tripled in length. A different person managing a small team managed each activity on the critical path, and each person provided a different excuse as to why their activity had a problem. Using the figure below and the clues, determine who was assigned to each activity and what they claimed was the problem causing the slippage.

Name: Andrea; Dora; Emily; Helen; John; Philip; Thomas

Problem: Bad Weather; Lack of Human Resources; Wrong Skill Level of Resources; Lack of Raw Materials; Wrong Raw Materials; Workers Out Sick; Breakdown in Equipment

Clues:

1. Helen's activity immediately followed the activity where workers had used the wrong lot of raw materials.
2. Activity 7 was assigned to a woman that had to deal with resources, namely lack of human resources, wrong skill level of resources, or human resources calling in sick.
3. Philip's problem, which was precipitated by bad weather, was with an activity that had an odd number assigned to it.
4. Andrea was not the person that had to deal with workers out sick.
5. Thomas managed the activity that immediately followed the activity where resources with the wrong skill level were assigned.

6. Activity 5 was where Emily had her problem.
7. John's problem, which did not involve a breakdown in equipment, occurred sometime after activity 2.
8. Activity 1, which was not Dora, started out poorly when the workers discovered that they had a lack of raw materials needed to complete the activity.

Hint: If you need help, another clue appears on p. 196.

Name_____ _____ _____

Problem_____ _____ _____

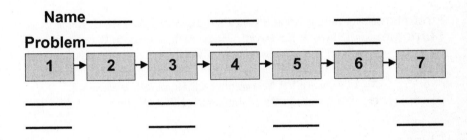

_____ _____ _____ _____

_____ _____ _____ _____

Logic Problem #64:
The Executive Levels _____

The top floor of the building in which Acme Corporation has its corporate headquarters has eight large offices, one for each of the executives. Using the figure below and the clues, determine the first name, surname, title, and office for each of the executives.

First Name: Conrad; Dora; Ethan; Fred; Hubert; Juliett; Karl; Louis
Surname: Dilworth; Edgeworth; Hogsworth; Jenworth; Lensworth;
                 Nullworth; Pegworth; Woolworth
Title: President; Executive Vice President; Senior VP (and Legal
                 Counsel); VP Accounting; VP Human Relations; VP
                 Engineering; VP Manufacturing; VP Quality

Clues:

1. Dilworth's office was immediately across the hall from Juliett's office, which was adjacent to Conrad's office.
2. Fred's office was next to Pegworth's office, which was not the Executive Vice President's office.
3. The Senior VP, who was not Juliett, had an office at one end of a row but not directly opposite Fred's office.
4. Ethan was in office 607.
5. The VP for Manufacturing, who was not Louis, had an office immediately between Edgeworth and Conrad.
6. Dora, who had nothing to do with quality, was in an odd-numbered office directly across the hall from the VP for Accounting.

7. The Executive Vice President, who resided in office 606, was on the other side of the hall from Hubert Jenworth but not directly opposite.
8. Nullworth's office was adjacent to the office of the President.
9. Hogsworth was not immediately opposite the VP for Engineering.
10. Woolworth was in office 605.
11. The VP for Quality was Lensworth.

Hint: If you need help, another clue appears on p. 196.

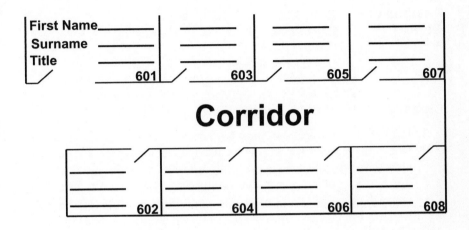

Logic Problem #65:
The Responsibility Assignment
Matrix (RAM) _____

The figure below is an open Responsibility Assignment Matrix form. Using the figure below and the clues, fill in the appropriate letters in the appropriate cells.

Assignments: R; R; R; R; R; A; A; C; C; I; I; I
Note: R = Responsibility
                   A = Approve
                   C = Coordinate
                   I = Inform

Clues:

1. Each of the work packages must have one and only one R assigned to it.
2. One of the three I's has an A immediately to the right of it, a C immediately to its left, and an R immediately below it.
3. The Sponsor column has an I in work package 4 with an A to its immediate left. The other two I's were for the same person. The sponsor also has only one other letter in the Sponsor column.
4. The APM for Cost has an R assigned for two of the work packages, as has the PM. The sponsor, as expected, has no R assigned.
5. One of the C's has an R to its immediate left; the other C has an R to its immediate right.
6. Work package 5 has only one R and one I assigned.
7. Work package 1 has only one letter assigned to it.

	PM	APM Cost	APM Quality	Sponsor
Work Package #1				
Work Package #2				
Work Package #3				
Work Package #4				
Work Package #5				

Logic Problem #66:
The Earned Value
Measurement Report _____

Below is an Earned Value Measurement report with 15 open entries. In each of
the entries, the numbers between $100 and $1500 appear in increments of
$100. Using the figure below and the clues, determine the location of each of
the 15 numbers.

Number: $100; $200; $300; $400; $500; $600; $700; $800; $900; $1000;
$1100; $1200; $1300; $1400; $1500

Clues:

1. For activity D, the magnitude of CV is greater than the magnitude of
   SV.
2. Reading down in the EV column, there is a $900 immediately below the
   $600 and a $1400 immediately below the $900.
3. Both activities A and B have favorable schedule variances but unfavorable cost variances; the cost variance for activity A is twice the cost
   variance for activity B.
4. Only one activity, which is not activity B, has an unfavorable schedule
   variance; the largest schedule variance in magnitude is $300; all of the
   cost variances fall between plus and minus $200.
5. Reading diagonally downward from left to right, there is $100, $1100,
   and $500 on one of the diagonals.

Activity	PV	EV	AC
A	_____	_____	_____
B	_____	_____	_____
C	_____	_____	_____
D	_____	_____	_____
E	_____	_____	_____

Logic Problem #67: The Family-Owned Business _____

You are a Project Manager who just accepted a job in a company started up by members of your family. In the lobby of the building are hung six portraits of the six senior officers, all members of your family. Using the figure below and the clues, determine the name, title, and relationship to you of each of the people represented in the six portraits.

Name: Jeff; John; Jane; Jenny; Jessica; Joseph

Title: President; VP Finance; VP Manufacturing; VP Quality; VP Information Systems; VP Engineering

Relationship: Mother; Father; Brother; Sister; Sister; Uncle

Clues:

1. Jeff's portrait is hanging adjacent to the VP for Quality.
2. The President's portrait is hung immediately to the right of your uncle's portrait.
3. Jenny's portrait is hung between the VP for Engineering and your uncle's portrait.
4. The VP for Manufacturing is Jessica.
5. One of your sister's portraits is positioned immediately below the VP for Information Systems.
6. The portrait of your sister Jane is positioned in the bottom row.
7. Your mother's portrait, which is in an even-numbered position, is immediately to the left of John's portrait.
8. Your father, who is not Joseph, is in position 6.

Hint: If you need help, another clue appears on p. 196.

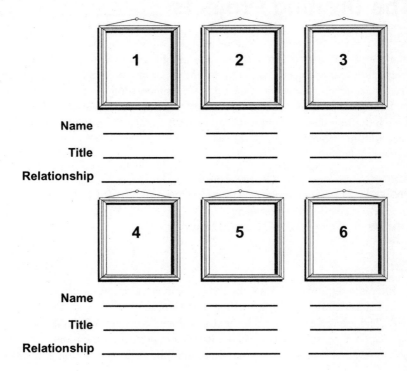

Name _____ _____ _____

Title _____ _____ _____

Relationship _____ _____ _____

Name _____ _____ _____

Title _____ _____ _____

Relationship _____ _____ _____

Logic Problem #68:
The Drafting Projects _____

Four people experienced in drafting were assigned to four projects for four companies. Each project required a different number of days to be completed. The four drafting people sat at the end of a long corridor as shown in the figure below. Using the clues and the figure, determine the name of each person at each drafting desk, the project they worked on, and the estimated time for each drafting project.

Name: Adam; Bob; George; Helen
Project: Prince Company; Robertson Company; Swift Company;
               Wellington Company
Time: 2 days; 3 days; 4 days; 5 days

Clues:

1. Adam required less time than the person working on the project for Prince Company but more time than George.
2. The job requiring two days was positioned between Adam on one side and the person working on the Robertson project on the other.
3. The person at position A required more time than the person at position C.
4. George, who is not working on the Prince project, is in position C, and the project for Swift Company is in position B.
5. The sum of the hours in position D, which is not Bob, and position B is eight hours.

Hint: If you need help, another clue appears on p. 196.

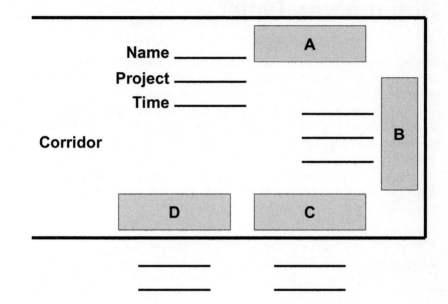

Logic Problem #69: Hiring a New PMP® _____

A company had a vacancy in one of the project management groups. One of the requirements was that the individual be a PMP® and have at least six years of experience working on high-technology project teams.

Six applicants, three men and three women, applied for the job. The first round of interviews was simply to review the resumes and see which applicants were qualified to go through the second round of interviews. All six applicants showed up at the same time for their short preliminary screening interview. Using the figure below and the clues, determine the position of each applicant, their name, the item of major strength in their resume, and the order in which they were interviewed.

Name: Cordell; Dell; Fiona; Gertrude; Harriett; Thomas

Strength: Ability to Work with People; Planning Skills; Cost Savings; Quality Improvement Efforts; Customer Satisfaction; Managing Multiple Projects

Order: 1st; 2nd; 3rd; 4th; 5th; 6th

Clues:

1. As you look at the figure, Dell is positioned two places to the right of the person with strength in managing multiple projects.
2. Only one person happened to be positioned in the order in which they were interviewed; this was not Fiona.
3. Gertrude was interviewed some time prior to the person whose resume emphasized quality improvement efforts, but not necessarily immediately before.
4. The woman in position 5 in the figure prepared a resume that emphasized an ability with cost savings.
5. Harriett, who was the last person to be interviewed, is positioned two places to the left of the first person to be interviewed and immediately to the left of the person whose strength on the resume appeared to be planning skills.

6. Position 1 in the figure is Cordell, who was interviewed immediately before the person who emphasized customer satisfaction skills and sometime after the person whose resume emphasized ability to work with people.
7. The person in position 3 was the fourth person to be interviewed.
8. Thomas was not in position 4.

Hint: If you need help, another clue appears on p. 196.

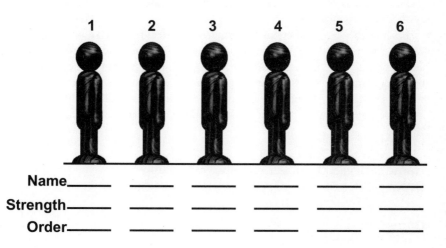

| 1 | 2 | 3 | 4 | 5 | 6 |

Name____ ____ ____ ____ ____ ____
Strength____ ____ ____ ____ ____ ____
Order____ ____ ____ ____ ____ ____

Logic Problem #70:
Working during
Plant Closing _____

A company usually closes its plant for the week between Christmas and New Year. This year, however, because of problems on one of the projects, the plant had to remain open for manufacturing so that the customer's scheduled delivery could be maintained.

Each of the six members of the project team decided to give up one day of vacation to be available for in-company support for the manufacturing personnel. Six cards were placed in a hat, each card containing one of the numbers between 26 and 31. Each of the six people then selected one of the cards to see which date they would work. Using the figure below and the clues, determine the order in which the people selected the cards and which date they worked.

Name: Eddie; Grant; Harry; Paula; Phyllis; Willy
Date: Dec. 26; Dec. 27; Dec. 28; Dec. 29; Dec. 30; Dec 31

Clues:

1. The fourth person to select a card was hoping that he could leave early to attend the New Year's Eve party at his neighbor's house; this was the day after Paula was scheduled to work.
2. The first person to draw a card did not have to work on the 27th.
3. Eddie, who followed Harry in the drawing, ended up working the day after Phyllis; the person who followed him in the card selection process worked later in the week.

4. Grant was the fifth person to select a card.
5. Phyllis selected a card immediately before the person who had to work on the day after Christmas.

Hint: If you need help, another clue appears on p. 196.

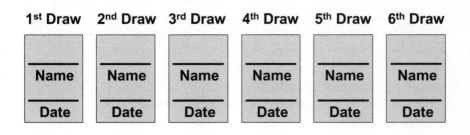

Logic Problem #71:
The Quality Problem _____

The project sponsor convened a meeting with the Project Manager, the Assistant Project Manager (APM) for Quality, and the APM for Cost to discuss the quality problem and to estimate the cost of correcting the problem. Using the figure below and the clues, determine the name and title of the person that sat in each seat and their estimate of the cost to correct the quality problem.

Name: Dolores; John; Ned; Paula
Title: Executive Sponsor; Project Manager; APM Cost; APM Quality
Cost: $20K; $25K; $30K; $35K

Clues:

1. The Project Manager was not the person who estimated $30K to correct the problem.
2. Ned was sitting at the table opposite the APM for Quality, who estimated the lowest cost to correct the problem.
3. Dolores, the APM for Cost Control, was sitting in a seat numbered two higher than the person who had the greatest estimate to correct the quality problem.
4. Paula sat in seat 4.
5. The person in seat 3 estimated $25K to correct the problem.

Hint: If you need help, another clue appears on p. 196.

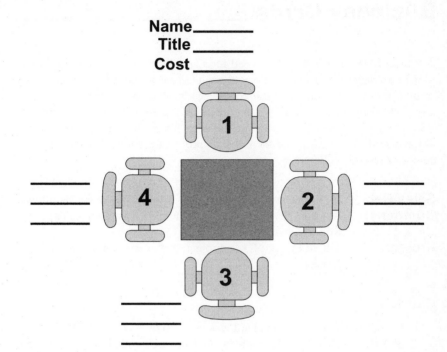

Logic Problem #72:
Business Cards _____

A Project Manager has an urgent need for a small quantity of chemicals. The Project Manager opens his directory of business cards and finds four business cards from four different chemical companies located on the same page in his directory. Using the figure below and the clues, for each business card determine the name of the sales representative in each chemical company, the name of the chemical company, and the previous project for which this chemical company provided chemicals.

Sales Rep.:   Alex Baker; Carol Demmings; Edward Fogle; Henry Ithica
Company: Aramis Chemicals; Novelis Chemicals; Paragon Chemicals; Rollins Chemicals
Project: Jolliett Project; Klein Project; Newman Project; Porthas Project

Clues:

1. Carol Demmings' business card was in position 3 in the directory.
2. The business card for the company that supplied chemicals for the Klein Project was positioned immediately above the card from Paragon Chemicals, whose sales rep was Edward Fogle.
3. Novelis Chemicals supplied chemicals previously for the Porthas Project.
4. Alex Baker, who does not work for Rollins Chemicals, supplied his company's chemicals for the Jolliett Project.
5. The business card in position 4 was not related in any way to the Newman Project.

Hint: If you need help, another clue appears on p. 196.

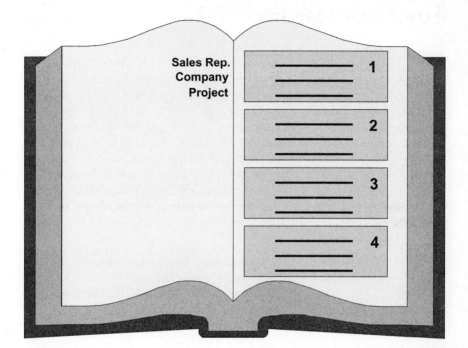

Logic Problem #73:
The Textbook Auction _____

A PMI® chapter found a way to raise money at each of its chapter meetings. Textbook authors donated copies of their recently published textbooks to the chapter. The textbooks were wrapped in paper so that nobody could see the title of the book or the author. The people at the chapter meeting were then told what project management subject the book covered, and then the books were auctioned off to the highest bidders where each bid had to be in multiples of $5 increments. Each book was auctioned off for a different amount.

Using the figure below, where the the books are positioned in the order in which they were auctioned off, and the clues, determine the subject of the book in each position, the name of the highest bidder, and the amount of money the chapter received for the book.

Subject: Advanced Project Management; Risk Management; Portfolio Management; Project Management Office
Winner: Jane Aston; Peggy Frummel; Neville Marsh; Paul Wadsworth
High Bid: $45; $50; $55; $60

Clues:

1. The book that Neville Marsh received was earlier in the auction than the book on risk management.
2. The book in position 4 was auctioned off for less money that the book describing the use of a project management office.
3. The book to be auctioned off first did not go for exactly $50.
4. The book that Jane Aston successfully bid on was immediately before the book that went for $55, which happened to be the book on portfolio management of projects.
5. The book on advanced project management was auctioned off for $5 less than the book received by Paul Wadsworth; the latter was auctioned off prior to the former.
6. The book in position 3 was auctioned off for more than $50.

Hint: If you need help, another clue appears on p. 196.

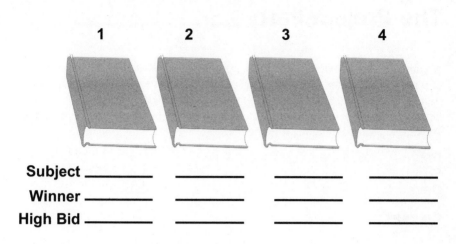

          1   2   3   4

Subject _____   _____   _____   _____

Winner _____   _____   _____   _____

High Bid _____   _____   _____   _____

Logic Problem #74:
The Project Party _____

A company has a custom that a party accompanies the successful completion
of a project where the Project Managers and Assistant Project Managers each
bring two types of food for the party: one main food group and one dessert.
Using the figure below and the clues, determine the office of each person and
which two foods they brought to the party.

PM: Anthony; Megan; Polly; Wally
Food: Chicken; Meat Casserole; Pasta; Stuffed Peppers
Dessert: Assorted Cheeses; Cake; Cookies; Ice Cream

Clues:

1. The person who brought the pasta as a main course, who does not occupy office 304, also brought the ice cream.
2. Anthony's office number is two higher than the person that brought the
   cookies.
3. Megan, who brought the meat casserole, has her office on the same side
   of the corridor as the person that brought the cake for dessert.
4. The person that occupies office 306 brought the assorted cheeses.
5. The person that occupies office 302, which is not Polly, brought a
   chicken dish for one of the main courses.

Hint: If you need help, another clue appears on p. 196.

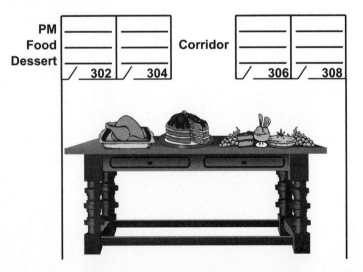

Logic Problem #75: Recognizing the New Chapter Officers _____

At a local chapter meeting of the Project Management Institute, four people stood up to be recognized as part of the core officer team for the upcoming year.

The figure below shows the four people. Using the figure and the clues, determine the full name of each officer, the company they work for, and their position in the figure.

First Name: Archie; Basil; Charlene; Denise
Surname: Evert; Flowers; Grant; Heinz
Company: Pongo Corp.; Richter Co.; Triton Corp.; Unger Co.

Clues:

1. The person in position 3 works for Triton Corp.
2. The person in position 4 is surnamed Grant.
3. Archie, who is not in position 2, is from Richter Co.
4. Denise is positioned immediately between the person from Unger Co. and the person surnamed Evert.
5. Basil is not in the first position.
6. Charlene is positioned somewhere to the right of Heinz.

Hint: If you need help, another clue appears on p. 196.

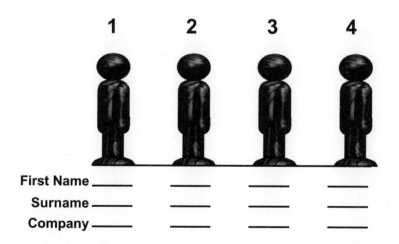

	1	2	3	4
First Name	___	___	___	___
Surname	___	___	___	___
Company	___	___	___	___

Logic Problem #76:
The Company Picnic _____

At the annual company picnic, project teams compete with each other for prizes and recognition. Each team creates a logo or emblem representing their project or customer, and sweatshirts and tee shirts are purchased with the emblems on them. Using the figure below and the clues, for each emblem determine the symbol on the emblem, the colors in the emblem, and the name of the project team.

Team: Forman Team; Rockwall Team; Prentice Aerospace Team; Maximillian Satellite Team
Symbol: Five Stars; Crossed Swords; Lightning Bolts; Wolf
Colors: Red and White; Green and Yellow; Black and Orange; Purple and Blue

Clues:

1. The Forman project team selected five stars as its emblem.
2. The emblem in position 2 had crossed swords on it.
3. The colors purple and blue were not on the emblem in position 1, which was not the Rockwall team.
4. The lightning bolts were colored black and orange and were on an emblem positioned somewhere to the left of the Maximillian team's emblem.
5. The emblem for the Prentice Aerospace team appears between the emblem with the picture of a wolf on it and the emblem that was colored green and yellow.

Hint: If you need help, another clue appears on p. 196.

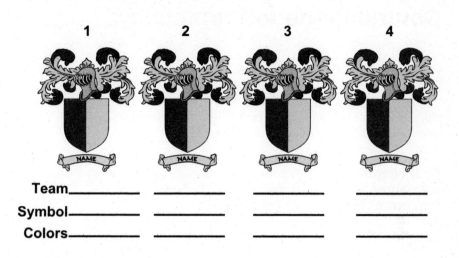

Team _____   _____   _____   _____

Symbol _____   _____   _____   _____

Colors _____   _____   _____   _____

Logic Problem #77:
Contributions to Profitability _____

Once a year, a small company recognizes the achievements of its Project Managers toward the profitability of the company. This year, four Project Managers were recognized for their contributions. Using the figure below and the clues, determine the full name of each Project Manager, their contribution to profitability, and their position in the figure.

First Name: Caroline; Kevin; Lucas; Lynn
Surname: Atkins; Denton; Harrison; Hill
Percent of Profits: 12%; 15%; 23%; 28%

Clues:

1. Harrison is in position 4.
2. Hill was told that the contribution was 23%.
3. Lynn's contribution was 15%.
4. Lucas is in position 2.
5. Kevin Atkins is somewhere to the right of the person with the greatest contribution.

Hint: If you need help, another clue appears on p. 196.

First Name _____   _____   _____   _____
Surname _____   _____   _____   _____
Profit,% _____   _____   _____   _____

Logic Problem #78:
On-the-Job Training _____

Six Project Managers were required to provide mentorship duties and on-the-job training for inexperienced workers who aspired to become Assistant Project Managers and eventually Project Managers. The training was being conducted in six different subjects although two of the six subjects are related. Using the figure below and the clues, determine the name of the Project Manager, name of the trainee, the subject of training, and their position.

Project Manager: Anderson; Caldwell; Guilliani; Herkens; James; Johnson
Trainee: Billings; Gumsy; Harwood; Ray; Trundwell; Urman
Subject: Cost Estimating; Cost Control; Engineering; Manufacturing; Procurement; Quality

Clues:

1. Harwood is the trainee in position 5.
2. Gumsy, who is not in position 3, is being trained to become the APM for Engineering.
3. Herkens is the Project Manager in position 2 but his trainee is not Billings.
4. The Project Manager in position 4, named James, is training in one of the two subjects involving cost; the other Project Manager training on cost is Caldwell.
5. The training for Manufacturing is in position 6.
6. Guilliani is being trained immediately between Procurement on one side and the trainee Trundwell on the other side.
7. Anderson and Ray are working together but not immediately to the left of the position where Urman is being trained.
8. Cost Estimating is the training subject at position 5.

Hint: If you need help, another clue appears on p. 196.

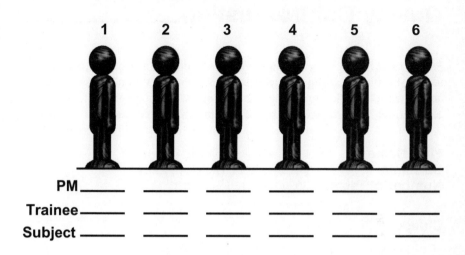

	1	2	3	4	5	6
PM	——	——	——	——	——	——
Trainee	——	——	——	——	——	——
Subject	——	——	——	——	——	——

Logic Problem #79:
Quality Control Testing _____

Four Project Managers were waiting for the results of their quality control testing. Each Project Manager requested that a different number of tests be conducted. Using the figure below and the clues, determine the full name of each Project Manager, the number of tests they requested, and their position.

First Name: Frank; Gregory; Ingrid; Paulette
Surname: Daniels; Froth; Graham; Pickler
Number of Tests: 30; 60; 90; 120

Clues:

1. Frank is two places to the left of Paulette Froth.
2. The person in position 1 did not request 90 tests.
3. Ingrid requested less than 90 tests; she is immediately to the right of the person surnamed Pickler.
4. The person in position 3, who is not Gregory, requested the most tests.
5. Graham requested 60 tests.

Hint: If you need help, another clue appears on p. 196.

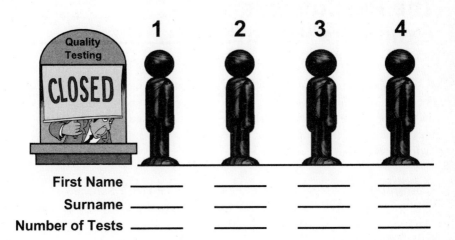

First Name _____   _____   _____   _____

Surname _____   _____   _____   _____

Number of Tests _____   _____   _____   _____

Logic Problem #80: The PM Software Exhibitors' Booths _____

Four companies purchased booths at a Project Management Convention in order to exhibit their new software. Each exhibitor had a special software product that they were promoting. Using the figure below and the clues, determine the position of each company, the name of their representative, and their special software product.

Company: Avron Software Corporation; Future Software
                        Company; Easy-to-Use Software Company; Business
                        Software Corporation
Representative: Blotto; Flowers; Iris; Tulip
Product: EVMS; Estimating; Scheduling; Best Practices
                        Libraries

Clues:

1. The representative surnamed Iris works for the Easy-to-Use Software Company.
2. The representative surnamed Flowers is in booth 1.
3. The representative surnamed Blotto is positioned immediately to the left of the Future Software Company booth, which does not have scheduling software.
4. The EVMS software is demonstrated in booth 2 and Avron Software specializes in Best Practices Libraries; the latter is two booths away from the Estimating software exhibit.

Hint: If you need help, another clue appears on p. 196.

Company _____   _____   _____   _____

Rep. _____   _____   _____   _____

Product _____   _____   _____   _____

Logic Problem #81: Planning Meetings versus Slippages _____

A company wanted to determine whether or not there was a relationship between the number of planning meetings and the size of the slippages on the projects. Five projects were analyzed, each headed up by a different Project Manager. Using the clues below and the figure, determine the first and last name of each Project Manager, the number of planning meetings they held, and the magnitude of the slippages.

Clues:

1. One project had the same number of planning meetings as slippages in weeks; this was neither Larry Franklin's project nor Barry's project.
2. Natalie had two planning meetings and Bellows had a six-week slippage; neither of these people had worked previously on any of the same projects with Anthony Ashcroft, who had five planning meetings.
3. Denise Richardson had a five-week slippage but required less than six planning meetings.
4. The three-week slippage had the most planning meetings.

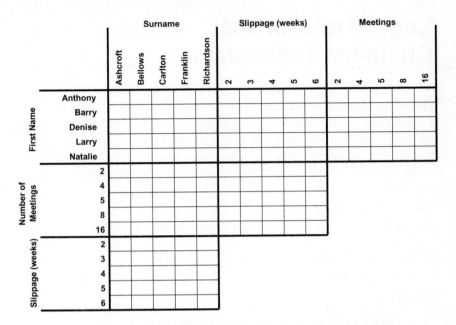

First Name	Surname	Slippage	Number of Meetings

Logic Problem #82:
Customer Presentations _____

On one bright Monday morning, all four conference rooms were in use by Project Managers for customer briefings. Each briefing was for a different customer and required different times. Using the figure below and the clues, determine the name of the Project Manager in each conference room, the name of the customer, and the amount of time needed for each presentation.

PM:　　　　Charles; George; Howard; Phillip

Company:　Grey Company; Green Company; Blue Company; White Company

Time:　　　2 hours; 3 hours; 4 hours; 5 hours

Clues:

1. The Green Company is being briefed in conference room 4.
2. The five-hour briefing is for White Company.
3. Phillip is conducting a briefing in conference room 3.
4. George is conducting a four-hour briefing; he is in the conference room adjacent to Howard.
5. The three-hour briefing is in conference room 2 but not for Blue Company.

Hint: If you need help, another clue appears on p. 196.

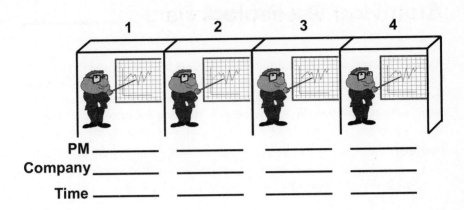

PM _____   _____   _____   _____

Company _____   _____   _____   _____

Time _____   _____   _____   _____

Logic Problem #83: Archiving the Project Data _____

As part of project closure, all project documentation is archived in filing cabinets. Each drawer in the two filing cabinets is assigned to one project that has recently been completed. Using the figure below and the clues, determine which project is assigned to which drawer in the filing cabinet.

Project: Castin Co.; Coltex Corp.; Delphino Co.; Eagle Products; Magnoflex Co.; Newton Corp.; Sandstone Industries; Tennadyne Corp.

Clues:

1. Newton Corporation drawer is immediately to the left of the Coltex drawer.
2. The Eagle Products drawer is two drawers below that of the drawer holding the Magnoflex Company documents.
3. The Castin Company drawer is positioned between the Tennedyne Corporation drawer, which is not one of the two top drawers, and the Sandstone Industries drawer.
4. The Delphino Company drawer is in drawer 6.

Hint: If you need help, another clue appears on p. 196.

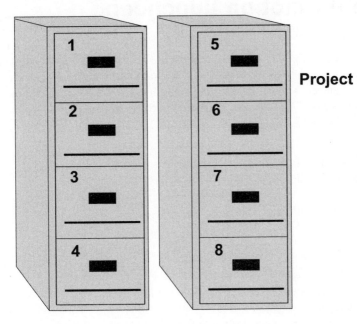

Project

Logic Problem #84:
The Promotion Luncheon _____

A company has a policy that when people are promoted to Project Management positions, three executives have a congratulatory luncheon with the new Project Manager. All four people are having lunch around the table shown in the figure below. Using the clues, determine the first name, surname, and title of the person in each seat.

First Name: Bob; Joseph; Paul; Carol
Surname: Phillips; Roth; Stedwell; Troff
Title: President; VP Project Management; VP Human Relations; Project Manager

Clues:

1. Paul is sitting in seat 1 and the VP for Project Management is in seat 4.
2. Bob, who is not surnamed Troff, is sitting opposite the new Project Manager.
3. Joseph was sitting opposite the President, who was sitting immediately to Roth's right.
4. Stedwell is the VP for Human Relations.

Hint: If you need help, another clue appears on p. 196.

First Name_____
Surname_____
Title_____

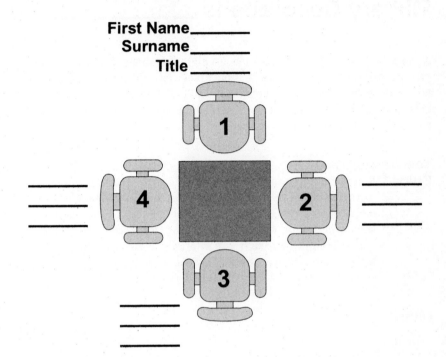

Logic Problem #85:
Military Decorations _____

A military Project Manager spent the last eight years managing military projects. In each of the eight years, the officer received a different military decoration. The decorations were mounted on a wall, as shown in the figure below. Using the figure below and the clues, determine the year and color of the award ribbon for each of the positions.

Year: 1999; 2000; 2001; 2002; 2003; 2004; 2005; 2006

Color: Red (for meritorious service in dealing with superiors); Orange (for meritorious service in managing scope changes); Yellow (for meritorious service in controlling costs); Green (for meritorious service in dealing with suppliers); Blue (for meritorious service in quality control); Purple (for meritorious service in dealing with stakeholders); Brown (for meritorious service in maintaining schedules); Black (for meritorious service in controlling risks)

Clues:

1. The award colored red is in position 2.
2. The award in position 3 was received in 2004.
3. The award received in 2006 is neither in position 5 nor in position 6, nor is it above or below the award received in 2000.
4. The award received in 2005 is positioned above the award colored black.
5. The award colored yellow is two positions to the left of the 2001 award (as you look at the awards) and immediately below the award that is colored purple.

6. The 2002 award, which was colored orange, is in the top row of awards.
7. The award colored blue is positioned immediately to the right of the award colored green as you look at the awards, and one of these two awards was received in 1999.

Hint: If you need help, another clue appears on p. 196.

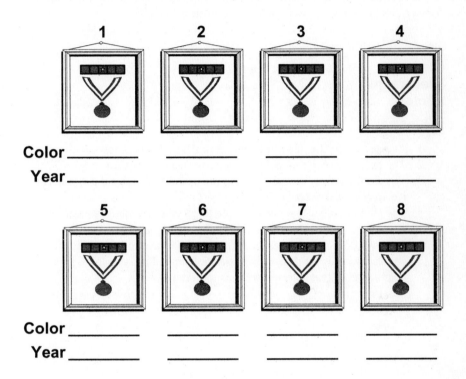

	1	2	3	4
Color	_____	_____	_____	_____
Year	_____	_____	_____	_____

	5	6	7	8
Color	_____	_____	_____	_____
Year	_____	_____	_____	_____

Logic Problem #86:
The Dinner Meeting _____

Once a month, four Project Management team members have dinner at a fine dining restaurant. Using the figure below and the clues, determine the entree, dessert, and beverage of each of the four Project Managers.

Entree:　　Steak; Chicken; Fish; Pasta
Dessert:　　Pie; Ice Cream; Fruit; Cheese
Beverage:　Wine; Coffee; Tea; Soda

Clues:

1. The dessert for the team member in position 2 was cheesecake.
2. The team member in position 3 preferred soda as beverage.
3. The team member that opted for pasta as a main course did not select ice cream for dessert.
4. The team member that chose coffee to go with the pie was positioned next to the person that chose fish as the main course.
5. As you look at the figure, the team member that chose steak as the main course and fruit for dessert is positioned immediately to the right of the team member that selected wine as a beverage.

Hint: If you need help, another clue appears on p. 197.

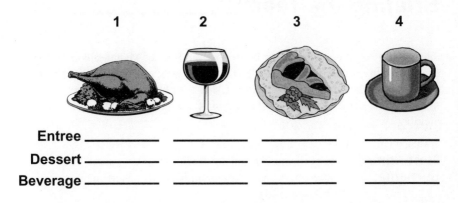

Entree _____ _____ _____ _____

Dessert _____ _____ _____ _____

Beverage _____ _____ _____ _____

Note: Artwork is not necessarily in the correct column.

Logic Problem #87:
Briefing the Team _____

Seven team members were being briefed by the Project Manager concerning changes to the original requirements. The position of each of the seven team members is shown in the figure below. Using the clues and the figure, determine the first name, surname, and position of each of the seven team members.

First Name: George; Henry; Kenneth; Kevin; Marcus; Paula; Tara
Surname: Anderson; Azure; Gustafson; Maloney; Merriman; Robertson; West

Clues:

1. Henry's seat number at the table is half that of Merriman's seat number.
2. Gustafson is in seat 2.
3. Robertson's seat number is three higher than Paula's seat number.
4. George is sitting at one end of the row, but Maloney does not have an end seat.
5. Marcus West is sitting in an odd-numbered seat.
6. Anderson, who is sitting in a higher seat number than Azure, has Kenneth sitting in the next seat either left or right.
7. The person in seat number 4 does not have the same first name or surname initial as any of the other team members.

Hint: If you need help, another clue appears on p. 197.

First Name ———————   ———————   ———————

Surname ———————   ———————   ———————

Logic Problem #88:
The Project Management
Golf Outing

During the company picnic, a golf tournament is held in which husband and wife teams must compete. This year, four Project Managers and their wives competed in the tournament. Using the figure below and the clues, determine the husband and wife teams, their position in the figure, and where they placed in the tournament.

Husband: Joseph; Lenny; Mickey; Neil
Wife: Bonnie; Carol; Selma; Zelda
Position: 1st; 2nd; 3rd; 4th

Clues:

1. The wife of the Project Manager in position 3 is Zelda.
2. The Project Manager in position 1 is Lenny.
3. The husband and wife team that came in fourth, which does not include Selma, is not in position 2.
4. The husband and wife team that came in second is in position 4; this is not the team of Neil and Carol.
5. Mickey and his wife placed third.

Hint: If you need help, another clue appears on p. 197.

	1	2	3	4
Husband				
Wife				
Position				

Logic Problem #89:
The Train Ride to Work _____

Five Project Managers take the same train each day to get from their homes into town. One morning, each of the five Project Managers brought with them a book to read for the long train ride. Each book was on a different project management subject and first published in a different year. Using the figure below and the clues, determine the time each person boarded the train, the book they were reading, and the year the book was published.

Time: 6:00 a.m.; 6:15 a.m.; 6:30 a.m.; 7:00 a.m.; 7:30 a.m.
Book: *Project Management Basics; Learning from Project Disasters; Earned Value Management; Risk Management; Scheduling Techniques*
Year: 2000; 2001; 2002; 2003; 3004

Clues:

1. The person reading *Earned Value Management* was sitting immediately to the right (as you look at the figure) of the person reading a book published in 2002.
2. The person that boarded the train at 6:00 a.m. was neither the person that was reading *Learning from Project Disasters* nor the person whose book was first published in 2003; the latter boarded the train later than the former.
3. The person who boarded the train at 6:15 a.m. was reading *Risk Management;* the person to his left was reading from a book first published in 2003.

4. The person who boarded at 7:00 a.m. was sitting to the immediate right of the person reading a book published in 2004, who in turn was sitting immediately to the right of the person reading *Learning from Project Disasters*.
5. The person who boarded the train at 6:30 a.m. sat immediately to the left of the person reading *Scheduling Techniques*.
6. The person reading a book first published in 2000 was sitting immediately to the right of the person who boarded the train at 7:30 a.m.
7. The person reading *Project Management Basics* sat between the person who boarded the train at 6:00 a.m. on his left and the person reading the book published in 2003 on his right.

Hint: If you need help, another clue appears on p. 197.

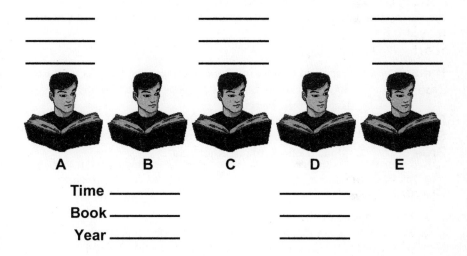

	A	B	C	D	E

Time ——— ———
Book ——— ———
Year ——— ———

Logic Problem #90:
The Six Sigma
Quality Awards _____

Once a quarter, the executive committee meets and selects a small number of employees that were deserving of Six Sigma Quality Awards during the past three months. Their pictures are then hung on the company's "Wall of Fame" for the next three months. Their pictures are hung on the wall according to their rank in the company. This quarter, five employees received quality awards; one division manager, two department managers, and two associates. Each of the employees received the awards for a different reason.

Using the figure below and the clues, determine the full name of each person, the reason they won the award, and the title of the project on which they worked.

Reason: Improved Quality in Manufacturing; Cost Savings from Less
            Scrap; Customer Satisfaction; New Product Development;
            Higher Profit Margins
First Name: Annette; Brad; Chloe; Gabriel; Inga
Surname: Bickerson; Korman; Lenso; Prince; Radway
Project: Alpha; Delta; Gamma; Rho; Zeta

Clues:

1. Lenso appears in picture 3.
2. Prince, who is not the person in picture 4 that developed techniques for improving customer satisfaction, headed up the Alpha Project.
3. Bickerson streamlined the paperwork system and received the award for higher profit margins.

4. Brad Korman is pictured on the same row as the Delta Project, which resulted in improved quality in manufacturing.
5. Annette's expertise and achievements are in new product development.
6. Gabriel's picture is positioned two lower than Inga's picture.
7. The Rho Project, which was not managed by Radway, is in position 5.
8. A department manager did not manage the Zeta Project.

Hint: If you need help, another clue appears on p. 197.

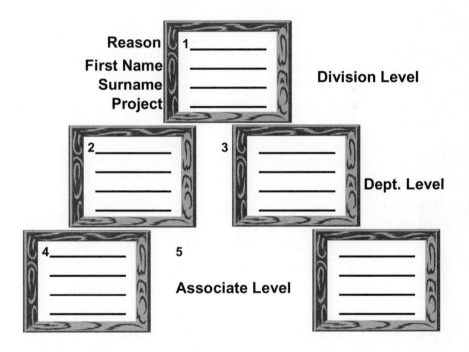

Logic Problem #91:
Talking about Retirement _____

Four Project Managers who had side-by-side offices as shown below were considering retirement. Each was a different pay grade and each had a different number of years to retirement. Using the figure and the clues below, determine the name of the Project Manager in each office, their pay grade, and the number of years left for retirement.

Name: Carol; David; Edith; Tom
Pay Grade: 6; 7; 8; 9
Years to Retirement: 1; 2; 3; 4

Clues:

1. As you look at the offices, David is immediately to the right of the person with four years to retire and immediately to the left of the pay grade 8.
2. Edith resides in office 3.
3. The person in office 2 has two years remaining before retirement.
4. The pay grade 6 has a higher office number than the pay grade 9.
5. Carol is not the pay grade 7 with one year to retirement.

Hint: If you need help, another clue appears on p. 197.

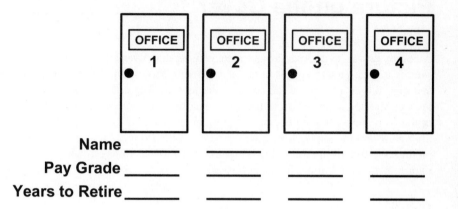

Name _____ _____ _____ _____

Pay Grade _____ _____ _____ _____

Years to Retire _____ _____ _____ _____

Logic Problem #92:
Picture on the Cover _____

A company was so good at project management that, over a five-month pe-
riod, five prestigious journals honored a different Project Manager each month
and placed their picture on the cover of the journal. The pictures of the five
Project Managers are shown in the figure below as they are hung in the lobby
of the company. The pictures are not hung in any specific order. Using the figure below and the clues, determine the name of the Project Manager in each
picture, the title of the journal that honored the Project Manager, and the
month in which the journal was published.

Name: Davin; Jenett; Nethrow; Sturgo; Vitmar
Journal: PM Universe; Management of Projects; PM Success; The World
              of Project Management; Applied Project Management
Month: February; March; April; May; June

Clues:

1. Davin, who is in position 2 in the figure, was not the first of the five
   to have his picture on a cover and did not appear in *Management of
   Projects*.
2. The Project Manager in position 3 was honored in March and the person
   in position 4 appeared in *PM Success*.
3. Nethrow's picture appeared two months after *Applied Project Management* honored a colleague.

4. *PM Universe* honored Jenett on the cover some time after Sturgo's picture appeared in another journal.
5. Vitmar's picture appeared in an earlier month than Sturgo's picture appeared.
6. *PM Universe,* which honored one of the project managers in April, is positioned to the left of the Project Manager who was honored in June, who is not in position 5.
7. *The World of Project Management* and *Management of Projects* honored two Project Managers in consecutive months, but not necessarily in this order.

Hint: If you need help, another clue appears on p. 197.

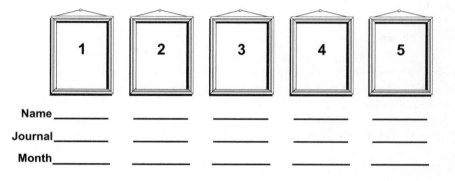

Name_____   _____   _____   _____   _____
Journal_____   _____   _____   _____   _____
Month_____   _____   _____   _____   _____

Logic Problem #93:
Using the Company Cars _____

A company has five company-owned cars that can be used by Project Managers to visit the job sites. Each of the cars is a different make and a different color. The five cars are parked in the spaces shown in the figure below. Using the figure and the clues, determine the make of each car in each position and the color.

Make: Chevy; Pontiac; Buick; Toyota; Mercury
Color: Blue; Black; Gray; Silver; White

Clues:

1. The car parked in space 3 is silver.
2. The Buick is parked in space 5.
3. The gray-colored car, which is not in space 5, is two spaces away from the Pontiac.
4. The blue-colored car is immediately to the left of the Toyota.
5. The Pontiac is the only General Motors car parked in the middle three spaces.
6. The Chevy is colored white.

Hint: If you need help, another clue appears on p. 197.

Make _____   _____

Color _____   _____

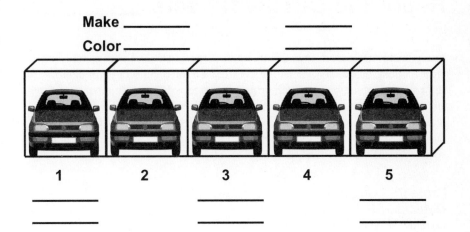

1   2   3   4   5

_____   _____   _____

_____   _____   _____

Logic Problem #94:
Reporting Quality Defects _____

Every Friday afternoon, four quality control specialists assigned to four large projects post the quality results for the week on the quality bulletin board shown in the figure below. Each project reported a different number of defects, and each Project Manager posted their results at a different time. Using the figure below and the clues, position each project, the number of defects, and the order in which they posted their results. The posting was not done in the same order as the positions on the bulletin board.

Project: Green Filter; Klondike; Manteen; Tribble
Defects: 2; 5; 6; 13
Order: First; Second; Third, Fourth

Clues:

1. The Manteen Project had five defects for the week.
2. The Project Manager that posted his results first had the most defects.
3. The project that reported six defects was posted immediately to the left of the Klondike report, which was posted immediately after it.
4. The third report to be posted was not in position 3.
5. Position 2 on the bulletin board, which was not the Green Filter Project, had a report posted on it some time prior to the posting on position 1, which did not have the fewest number of defects to report.

Hint: If you need help, another clue appears on p. 197.

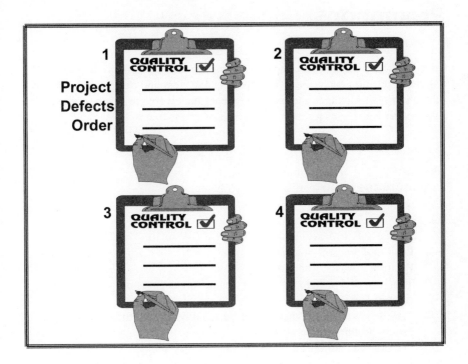

Logic Problem #95: Promotions _____

Four Project Managers were recently promoted. Using the figure below and the clues, position each of the four Project Managers and determine the name of each Project Manager, the month in which they were promoted, and their salary increase.

Name: Davis; Hollingsworth; Jerico; Klontis
Month: May; June; July; August
Pay Increase: 10%; 12%; 14%; 16%

Clues:

1. Position 2 was the June promotion.
2. Position 3 was Hollingsworth.
3. The 16% salary increase, which was in August, was immediately to the right of Davis.
4. May was not the month in which Jerico received his promotion, and Jerico did not receive 12%.
5. Position 4 is not the July promotion.
6. Klontis's pay increase was one month away from the person that received the 10% salary increase.

Hint: If you need help, another clue appears on p. 197.

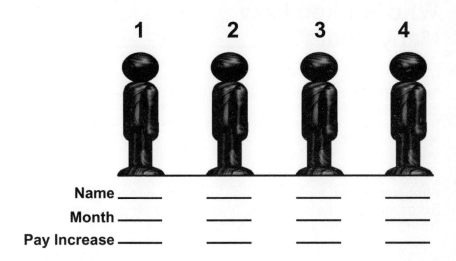

Name _____   _____   _____   _____
Month _____   _____   _____   _____
Pay Increase _____   _____   _____   _____

Logic Problem 96: Who Worked How Many Hours?

In the figure below are seven members of the project team that had been instrumental in making the project a success. Each team member worked a different number of hours over the past several months. Using the figure below and the clues, determine the full name of the person in each position and how many hours each one worked.

First Name: Elizabeth; Fred; Henry; Jordan; Mary; Nancy; Steven
Surname: Andrews; Carlsen; Dirkson; Netz; Parker; Storey; Villano
Hours: 260; 285; 451; 489; 590; 700; 860

Clues:

1. The person who worked 860 hours is two positions to the right of Carlsen.
2. The person with the next fewest hours from Carlsen is Jordan.
3. Villano is in position 3.
4. Elizabeth, who is positioned to the immediate right of the person that worked 700 hours, worked 451 hours; neither of these two people are surnamed Netz.
5. Henry, who worked an even number of hours but is not surnamed Dirkson, is in position 1 in the figure.

6. Mary is two positions to the left of Parker, the person who worked the fewest number of hours; Parker is positioned somewhat to the left of Andrews.
7. The person in position 6 worked 590 hours; the person positioned immediately to the right did not work either 451 or 489 hours.
8. Nancy Storey worked an odd number of hours and is positioned in an odd-numbered location.
9. Steven is not located in position 5.

Hint: If you need help, another clue appears on p. 197.

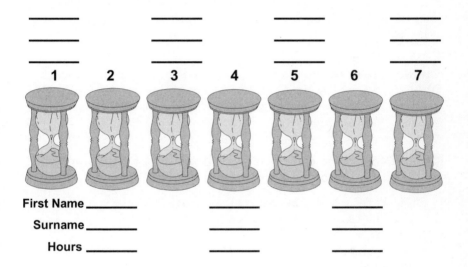

| | 1 | 2 | 3 | 4 | 5 | 6 | 7 |

First Name _____
Surname _____
Hours _____

Logic Problem #97:
The Team Meeting Seating
Arrangement _____

A company had a policy that the seating around a conference table for a project team meeting would be done according to perceived importance by the Project Manager. The people sitting closer to the Project Manager obviously were considered to be more important than those sitting further away.

In the figure below is a conference table for seven of the team members. Using the figure and the clues, determine the name and title of the person in each position.

Name: Brisco; Flanigan; Kirchoff; Nemens; Parsons; Watkins; Yelling
Title: Project Manager; APM Earned Value Measurement (EVMS); APM Engineering; APM Legal; APM Procurement; APM Manufacturing; APM Quality

Clues: (Note: Left and right are the seated person's left and right, not as you look at the figure.)

1. The Project Manager, as expected, was in seat 4; Brisco was not senior enough to be seated on either side of him.
2. Parsons occupied seat 3.
3. Yelling, who was not the Project Manager, was seated immediately to the left of the APM for EVMS, who had a higher seat number than the APM for Procurement.

4. The APMs for Engineering and Legal were seated equidistant from the Project Manager, with the former APM in a higher seat number than the latter APM.
5. Nemens did not occupy seat 5.
6. Watkins, the APM for Manufacturing, sat in an even-numbered seat.
7. Kirchoff was positioned in a seat numbered two higher than Flanigan.

Hint: If you need help, another clue appears on p. 197.

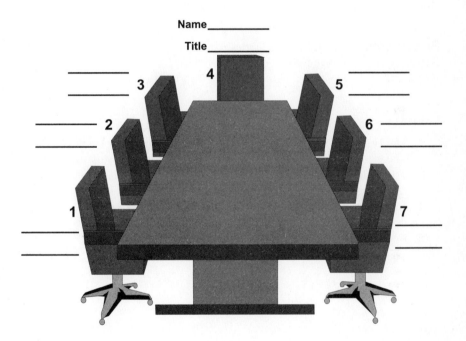

Logic Problem #98:
Raising Money for Charity _____

Once a year, project teams from the company participate in a fund-raising event for charity. This year, four project teams participated. Using the figure below and the clues, determine the full name of each Project Manager, the title of their project, and how they ranked with regard to raising money. In the figure, position 1 raised the most and position 4 raised the least.

First Name: April; Bryan; Charles; Germain
Surname: Morton; Spruce; Tripp; Wallace
Project: Cold Gas; Hot Gas; Liquefaction; Vaporization

Clues:

1. The Hot Gas Project raised the second greatest amount of funds.
2. The team managed by Charles raised the third greatest amount of funds.
3. Tripp's liquefaction project team, which did not raise the least amount, raised the next greatest amount than Germain's team.
4. April's team raised less money than the Vaporization Project team; neither of these involved Spruce.
5. Bryan is not surnamed Morton.

Hint: If you need help, another clue appears on p. 197.

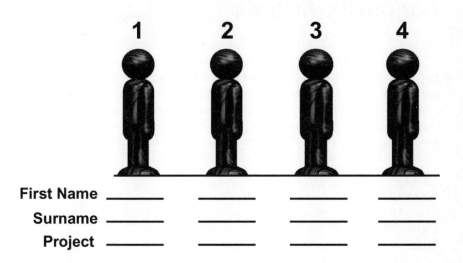

First Name _____   _____   _____   _____

Surname _____   _____   _____   _____

Project _____   _____   _____   _____

Logic Problem #99:
Longevity Awards _____

A small company decided to recognize the contribution of its employees that have been with the company for more than 10 years. Five Project Managers had been chosen to be the recipients of five different gifts for their years with the company. Each Project Manager had been with the company a different numbers of years and each received a different gift. Using the figure below, determine the full name of each Project Manager, the number of years they had been with the company, and the gift they received.

First Name: Amos; Bob; Darcy; Karl; Mary
Surname: Antine; Barbo; Charpel; Front; Robertson
Experience: 11 years; 12 years; 16 years; 19 years; 20 years
Gift: Watch; Sweater; Radio; Plant; Software

Clues:

1. Karl Antine, who was not the recipient of the watch, did not have 12 years of service.
2. The gift for 16 years of service was a woman's sweater, naturally given to a woman.
3. Charpel did not receive a plant for the 19 years of service.
4. Mary, who was not Robertson, had 16 years of service.
5. Darcy Barbo has been with the company the longest.
6. Front, who is not Bob and did not have 16 years of service, got the watch.
7. Amos received the software gift, which was not given for 12 years of service.
8. Bob and Robertson had been golf buddies for years.

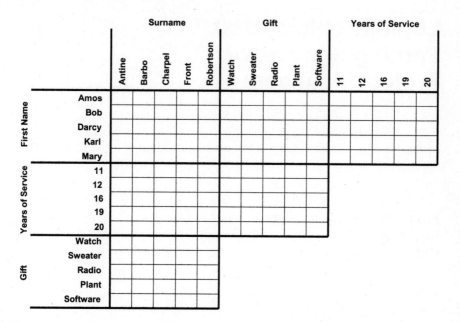

First Name	Surname	Experience	Gift

Logic Problem #100: Parking Spaces for Project Managers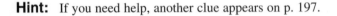

In a company, senior Project Managers were assigned parking spaces according to their seniority. Using the figure below and the clues, determine the full name of each Project Manager, the car they drove, and the position of their parking space.

First Name: John; Larry; Mary; Philip
Surname: Caster; Corwin; Eagleton; Germain
Car: Ford; General Motors; Chrysler; Toyota

Clues:

1. John's car was in space 3.
2. The Chrysler was parked to the immediate left of Larry Caster's car.
3. Mary's General Motors car was parked further to the right than Corwin's car, which was not a Ford.
4. Germain parked in space 2.

Hint: If you need help, another clue appears on p. 197.

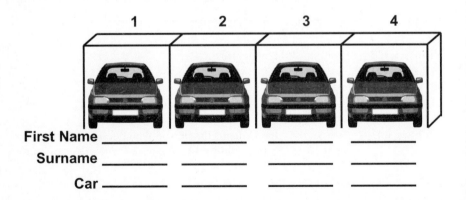

First Name _____   _____   _____   _____
Surname _____   _____   _____   _____
Car _____   _____   _____   _____

Additional Clues _____

Problem #3	First identify the title of the "grouch."
Problem #7	First locate the position of the book discussing the Professional Responsibility domain area.
Problem #8	First work out the name of the person in position 8.
Problem #15	Work out the department and then the name of the person in picture 6.
Problem #16	Determine the name of the Black Belt Project Manager in position 4.
Problem #17	Start by working out the color of David's package.
Problem #18	Work out the surname of the team member in position F. Then work out the area of responsibility for team member A.
Problem #19	Determine the name of the Project Manager in office A.
Problem #20	Determine Manning's title and then position Newton.
Problem #21	Find the title of the report in position 1.
Problem #22	Position Rose and then Kipple
Problem #32	Narrow the possible seat assignments for Frank and George and then position the APM for Design Engineering.
Problem #33	Position Bill in the figure.
Problem #34	First identify Gloria's team and then determine her qualifying score.
Problem #36	Locate the Quality office.
Problem #37	First position the Zeno award.
Problem #38	First locate Betty's position.
Problem #39	Identify Greenwood's first name and the briefcase selected.
Problem #40	Position Mulligan's office.
Problem #41	First locate the laboratory where the Epsilon Project is being tested.
Problem #42	First find the people sitting in each of the seats beginning with Frank.
Problem #43	First identify the name of the person who boards at 28th Street, then the title followed by the name of the person who boards at 230th Street.
Problem #44	Identify the name of the Project Manager in position 1.
Problem #45	First work out the size of Maxine's cost overrun and then her seat.
Problem #46	Find the floor that Becky works on and then the first name of the person in position 1 in line.

Problem #47	First work out Rex's area of expertise.
Problem #48	Work out Stevenson's company.
Problem #49	Find out which house Berger lives in and the color of the house.
Problem #50	Find the flight number and then the name of the Project Manager departing from gate 29.
Problem #51	Find out during which session on Wednesday the Initiation domain area was taught.
Problem #52	First work out the location of the red warehouse.
Problem #53	Determine the life-cycle phase covered in Bobbi's report and then the position on the desk.
Problem #54	Find the value of the gift received from the Minister of Trade.
Problem #57	Find Kerrie Pancoe's report preference.
Problem #58	Identify Bobbi's position.
Problem #59	Find Victor's seat at the table.
Problem #60	Find the color of the large cylinder in position D.
Problem #61	Work out Barbara's position.
Problem #62	Find the position of the workstation for the Grade 7.
Problem #63	First position Philip.
Problem #64	First position the VP for Manufacturing, then Dora, then Conrad.
Problem #67	Position Jenny, then Jeff.
Problem #68	Position the job requiring two days.
Problem #69	Find Harriett's position in the figure.
Problem #70	Determine who selected the fourth card.
Problem #71	Determine where Dolores was sitting.
Problem #72	First find Baker's company.
Problem #73	Find the subject and then the bid price for the book in position 1.
Problem #74	Determine who sits in office 302.
Problem #75	Determine which company is in position 2 and then solve for Denise's surname.
Problem #76	Identify which team is in position 1.
Problem #77	Find Kevin Atkin's location and profit percentage.
Problem #78	Find Guilliani's position.
Problem #79	Find the name of the person in position 3.
Problem #80	Determine the software for booth 4.
Problem #82	Position George's briefing.
Problem #83	Position the Coltex drawer.
Problem #84	Find the title of the person in seat 3.
Problem #85	First identify the position of the award colored purple.

Problem #86	First find out who ate the steak.
Problem #87	Determine the surname of the person is seat 4.
Problem #88	Position Neil and Carol.
Problem #89	Determine the book being read by person A.
Problem #90	First position Brad Korman.
Problem #91	Position David's office.
Problem #92	Determine the name of the person who appeared in February.
Problem #93	Identify the car in space 1 and then the color of the car is space 5.
Problem #93	First find the number of defects on the Klondike Project.
Problem #95	First position Davis.
Problem #96	Determine how many hours Henry worked, then position Mary.
Problem #97	Find the names of the people in position 5, then 4, then 1.
Problem #98	Find out how much money Germain's team raised (i.e., position).
Problem #100	Find out who parked in space 1.

Solutions

Problem #1

Bob; status report; neutral; 3 pages
John; progress report; unfavorable; 4 pages
Karen; forecast report; favorable; 5 pages

Problem #2

Position 1; Paul; CPIF
Position 2; Alice; CPFF
Position 3; Richard; FFP
Position 4; Frank; CPPC
Position 5; Jane; T&M
Position 6; Tim; FPIF

Problem #3

Position 1; Fred; Electrical Engineer; 21 years of experience
Position 2; Bob; Mechanical Engineer; 10 years of experience
Position 3; Henry; Project Manager; 14 years of experience
Position 4; Louis; Assistant Project Manager; 17 years of experience

Problem #4

Andrew Edgewater; $50K; Wrong People
Bob Denton; $300K; Faulty Equipment
Carol Ashcroft; $200K; Bad SOW
David Carlton; $10K; Bad Estimates
Edgar Bonds; $100K; Poor Quality

Problem #5

Adam Monroe; Scope Management; 12 hours
Brian Jones; Communications Management; 14 hours
Carol Norwood; Time Management; 10 hours
Diane Wilson; Cost Management; 16 hours
Edward Smith; Risk Management; 8 hours

Problem #6

Bill; Manufacturing; Yellow; Theatre Tickets
Frank; Accountant; Purple; Company Car
Gerald; Project Manager; Blue; Sports Event Tickets
Norman; Quality; Green; Dinner
Melissa; Engineering; Red; Time Off

Problem #7

Position 1; Planning; 95 pages; Black
Position 2; Initiation; 100 pages; Green
Position 3; Professional Responsibility; 105 pages; White
Position 4; Execution; 90 pages; Red
Position 5; Closure; 120 pages; Yellow
Position 6; Control; 80 pages; Purple

Problem #8

Position 1; William; PMO Manager
Position 2; Florence; Portfolio Management of Projects
Position 3; Karen; EPM
Position 4; Thomas; PMIS
Position 5; John; Mentorship
Position 6; Nellie; Benchmarking
Position 7; Roger; PM Tools
Position 8; Mollie; Six Sigma Monitoring

Problem #9

Activity	Duration	ES	EF	LS	LF
A	3	0	3	4	7
B	7	0	7	0	7
C	5	0	5	2	7
D	2	7	9	11	13
E	6	7	13	7	13
F	1	5	6	12	13
G	4	13	17	13	17

Problem #10

Activity	PV	EV	AC
A	100	0	0
B	100	150	90
C	140	200	140
D	280	380	300
E	80	200	220
	===	===	===
	700	930	750

Problem #11

Anthony Richardson; Beta Company; Cost Overrun
Barry Ashcroft; Gamma Company; Quality
Denise Carlton; Epsilon Company; Faulty Equipment
Larry Bellows; Delta Company; Bad Statement of Work
Natalie Franklin; Alpha Company; No People

Problem #12

PM	Session I	Session II	Session III
Andrews	Chicago	Boston	Pittsburgh
Bellows	Pittsburgh	Denver	Los Angeles
Carlton	Los Angeles	Pittsburgh	Denver
Daily	Boston	Los Angeles	Chicago
Lyndhurst	Denver	Chicago	Boston

Daily had the most frequent flier miles.

Problem #13

Activity	Duration	ES	EF	LS	LF
A	4	0	4	1	5
B	2	0	2	3	5
C	5	0	5	0	5
D	3	2	5	9	12
E	7	5	12	5	12
F	6	5	11	6	12
G	1	12	13	12	13

The critical path is 13 weeks. Activity F has an early finish time of 11 weeks, but activity F cannot be on the critical path because there is only one critical path and activity E is on the critical path. Therefore, activity G must have a duration of 1 week. We now know the ES, EF, LS, and LF for activity E. Because activity F has an EF of 11 weeks, the durations of activities C and F must be 11 weeks, and therefore 5 and 6 weeks. Activity C must be 5 weeks to align with the ES of 5 in activity E. If activity C were 6 weeks in duration, the length of the critical path could not be 13 weeks. Using clue 3 and knowing that the LF of activity D must be 12 weeks, the duration of activity D must be 3 weeks. Using clue 4, which tells us that activity A has only 1 week of slack, and knowing that the LF for activity A is 5 weeks, the duration of activity A must be 4 weeks.

Problem #14

Activity	Duration	ES	EF	LS	LF
A	3	0	3	4	7
B	7	0	7	0	7
C	5	0	5	2	7
D	2	7	9	11	13
E	6	7	13	7	13
F	1	5	6	12	13
G	4	13	17	13	17

From the clues, activities A, C, and E have slack. Activity F must also have slack since activity C is on a path with it. Therefore, the critical path must be B–D–G. Since activity C has 8 weeks of slack, activity F must also have 8 weeks of slack, which means, by elimination, that activity A has 6 weeks of slack and the duration for activity A must be 4 weeks. From clue 1, the critical path, which must have three and only three activities in it, must be the numbers 5, 6, and 7, and equal to 18 weeks. From clue 5, the duration for activity F must be 3 weeks and activity C must be 1 week. Therefore, activity E must be 2 weeks in duration. Now we can calculate the ES, EF, LS, and LF for activities C and F. Since the length of the critical path is 18 weeks, we now know that the duration of activity G must be 6 weeks. After calculating the ES, EF, LS, and LF for activity E, we know that the duration of activity B must be 7 weeks.

Problem #15

Position 1; Olive; Marketing
Position 2; Daniel; Accounting
Position 3; Kenneth; Engineering
Position 4; Nadine; R&D
Position 5; Alice; Information Systems
Position 6; Steven; Sales
Position 7; Hilda; Manufacturing

Problem #16

Position 1; Carol; Industrial Engineering; $100K
Position 2; Denise; Electrical Engineering; $1M
Position 3; Amos; Mechanical Engineering; $500K
Position 4; Barry; Civil Engineering; $200K

Problem #17

Position 1; Barbara; Pink
Position 2; Edward; Green
Position 3; Francine; Brown
Position 4; Andrea; Yellow
Position 5; Charlie; Blue
Position 6; David; White
Position 7; Gwen; Beige
Position 8; Harry; Black

Problem #18

Position A; Paula Dante; Engineering
Position B: Frank Jennings; Quality
Position C; David Edwards; Safety
Position D; Steven Newman; Cost
Position E; Jeanie Springer; Software
Position F; Naomi Gamble; Manufacturing

Problem #19

Office A; Bellows; grade 7; $5M
Office B; Caruso; grade 9; $3M
Office C; Adams; grade 6; $4M
Office D; Davidson; grade 8; $2M

Problem #20

Office A; Bob Robinson; Project Manager
Office B; Alicia Parson; Junior Engineer
Office C; Denise Manning; Senior Engineer
Office D; Charles Newton; Engineer

Problem #21

Position 1; Poltex
Position 2; Blue Spectrum

Position 3; Low Density
Position 4; Phoenix
Position 5; Red Prism
Position 6; Spiral
Position 7; Low Texture

Problem #22

Position 1; Edgar Kipple; 150
Position 2; Rose Oswald; 160
Position 3; Julie Monroe; 180
Position 4; Tom Lancaster; 165
Position 5; Frieda North; 140
Position 6; Howard Pierce; 170

Problem #23

Alfonso; Execution; 5; 3
Dirk; Management Plan; 15; 1
Maggie; Develop Charter; 12; 2
Quinton; Scope Statement; 10; 2.5
Susan; Monitor and Control; 8; 1.5

Problem #24

Alfonso; Scope Definition; 6; 6
Dirk; Scope Control; 9; 3
Maggie; Scope Planning; 8; 5
Quinton; Verification; 5; 4
Susan; Create WBS; 7; 2

Problem #25

Alfonso; Schedule Development; 8; 6
Dirk; Activity Definition; 15; 5
Maggie; Resource Estimating; 10; 3
Quinton; Duration Estimating; 12; 4
Susan; Sequencing; 20; 7

Problem #26

Alfonso; Budgeting; 15; 12
Dirk; Control; 20; 9
Maggie; Estimating; 10; 6

Problem #27

Alfonso; Risk Planning; 15; 10
Dirk; Quantitative Analysis; 10; 14
Maggie; Response Planning; 20; 16
Quinton; Qualitative Analysis; 30; 12
Susan; Risk Identification; 25; 8

Problem #28

Alfonso; Plan Purchases; 35; 8
Dirk; Responses; 25; 4
Maggie; Select Sellers; 20; 6
Quinton; Plan Contracting; 30; 10
Susan; Contract Administration; 10; 3

Problem #29

Alfonso; Human Resource Planning; 14; 6
Dirk; Develop Team; 15; 4
Maggie; Acquire Team; 10; 5
Quinton; Manage Team; 12; 3

Problem #30

Alfonso; Manage Stakeholders; 6; 4
Dirk; Communications Planning; 10; 5
Maggie; Information Distribution; 12; 3
Quinton; Performance Reporting; 8; 2

Problem #31

Alfonso; Planning; 30; 8
Dirk; Control; 20; 12
Maggie; Assurance; 25; 10

Problem #32

Seat 1; Louise Vixen; Project Manager
Seat 2; Irma Stippends; Piping Engineering
Seat 3; Frank Williams; Civil Engineering
Seat 4; Kathy Quade; Mechanical Engineering
Seat 5; Hamilton Roberts; Cost Control
Seat 6; George Parker; Design Engineering
Seat 7; Julie Unger; Quality Assurance

Problem #33

Booth A; Francine; Bristol Co.
Booth B; Alan; Colgate Co.
Booth C; Gwen; Devlin Co.
Booth D; Harry; Wallace Co.
Booth E; Bill; Egret Co.
Booth F; Ellen; Turball Co.

Problem #34

Blue team on the left side of the quizmaster
David; 193; Captain
Gloria; 192
Barbara; 191
Frank; 197
Red team on the right side of the quizmaster
Christine; 190; Captain
Alan; 195
Howard; 196
Elisa; 194

Problem #35

1:00 p.m.; Alfred Graham; Mechanical Engineer
2:00 p.m.; David Edwards; Manufacturing Engineer
3:00 p.m.; Bob Franklin; Civil Engineer
4:00 p.m.; Carl Hill; Electrical Engineer

Problem #36

Office 1; Engineering; Barry Wilson; Eileen Newman
Office 2; Manufacturing; Iggy Stone; Gertrude Maxwell
Office 3; Quality; Andrew Pringle; Cedric Richardson
Office 4; Scheduling; Joseph Oregon; Dora Vargo
Office 5; Accounting; Frank Turner; Henrietta Quiggly

Problem #37

Position 1; Edgewood; Superior Overall Performance
Position 2; Zeno; Customer Support
Position 3; Argotech; Product Design
Position 4; Ducor; Low-Cost Production
Position 5; Botson; Ten Years of Partnership Excellence
Position 6; Mowtex; Product Quality

Position 7; Wilson; Technology Breakthrough
Position 8; Chilling; On-Time delivery

Problem #38

Box 1; Steven; $1500
Box 2; Wade; Stereo
Box 3; John; Gift Certificate
Box 4; Dora; $1000
Box 5; Betty; Management Granted Time Off
Box 6; Carol; Use of the Company Car

Problem #39

Briefcase 1; Gerald Norwell; Boston
Briefcase 2; Evelyn Greenwood; Miami
Briefcase 3; Richard Davis; Chicago
Briefcase 4; Mark Hampton; Denver
Briefcase 5; Florence Powell; Phoenix

Problem #40

Office 1; Pullman; R&D
Office 2; Hendrix; Manufacturing
Office 3; Jackson; Quality
Office 4; Mulligan; Marketing
Office 5; Sommerville; Information Technology
Office 6; Nixon; Engineering

Problem #41

Lab 1; Delta; 1 hour
Lab 2; Alpha; Test completed
Lab 3; Gamma; 2 hours
Lab 4; Epsilon; 1.5 hours
Lab 5; Beta; 2.5 hours

Problem #42

Seat 1; Gus; Project Management
Seat 2; Charles; Cost
Seat 3; Kathy; Technical Approach
Seat 4; Victor; Previous Performance
Seat 5; Phil; Previous Performance
Seat 6; Paul; Technical Approach

Seat 7; Rachael; Cost
Seat 8; Lori; Project Management
Seat 9; Steve; Cost
Seat 10; Frank; Previous Performance
Seat 11; Carol; Project Management
Seat 12; Louis; Technical Approach
Seat 13; Richard; Technical Approach
Seat 14; Gilda; Project Management
Seat 15; David; Past Performance
Seat 16; Paula; Cost

Problem #43

230th Street; Alex; Procurement Specialist
175th Street; Edward; Design Engineer
110th Street; Carla; Project Manager
70th Street; Barbara; Cost Accountant
28th Street; Paul; Quality Assurance Specialist

Problem #44

Position 1; Neville; Yarmouth; 100
Position 2; Prince; Convex; 600
Position 3; Reynolds; Apex; 800
Position 4; McGill; Dixon; 200
Position 5; Bosworth; Quartz; 350

Problem #45

Seat 1; Jerry; Bad Weather; $50K
Seat 2; Maxine; Inexperienced Workers; $60K
Seat 3; Sandra; Equipment Breakdown; $70K
Seat 4; Ned; Wrong Materials; $40K

Problem #46

Position 1; Andrea Glass; 3rd floor
Position 2; Charlene Imwell; 2nd floor
Position 3; Becky Hendrix; 1st floor
Position 4; Denise Fiorella; 4th floor

Problem #47

Office 405; Hilda; Earned Value Measurement; 20 years
Office 406; Susan; Quality; 22 years

Office 407; Rex; Engineering; 25 years
Office 408; George; Manufacturing; 15 years

Problem #48

2002; Stevenson; President; Dalpro
2003; Wilson; VP Project Management; Boomer
2004; Merriman; VP Engineering; Alcax
2005; Richardson; VP Information Systems; Condiphor

Problem #49

House 121; Berger; White, 1 Child
House 122; Adams; Brown; 3 Children
House 123; Chalmers; Blue; 0 Children
House 124; Davidson; Black; 2 Children
House 125; Edgewater; Gray; 4 Children

Problem #50

Gate 28; Anderson; Los Angeles; 2044
Gate 29; Wylie; Chicago; 581
Gate 30; Wellington; Denver; 604
Gate 31; Bellman; Detroit; 1023

Problem #51

Monday; Control; Execution; Planning; Closure; Initiation; Professional Responsibility
Tuesday; Closure; Initiation; Control; Professional Responsibility; Execution; Planning
Wednesday; Planning; Professional Responsibility; Execution; Control; Closure; Initiation

Problem #52

Position 1; Heppy; White; 400,000 square feet
Position 2; Collins; Red; 160,000 square feet
Position 3; Bell; Green; 280,000 square feet
Position 4; Wells; Black; 80,000 square feet

Problem #53

Position 1; Agnes; Salary Deductions; Execution
Position 2; Bobbi; Shipping; Requirements Definition

Position 3; Ethel; Estimating; Detailed Planning
Position 4; Thomas; Benefits; Preliminary Planning

Problem #54

Position 1; Coat, Minister of Trade; $600
Position 2; Statue; Minister of Economic Development; $300
Position 3; Picture; Minister of Education; $1000
Position 4; Vase; Minister of Finance; $200

Problem #55

Andrew Burrows; 5 days; September
Bridget Anderson; 15 days; May
Dennis Stephanovic; 10 days; June
Frank Clearington; 8 days; July
Vanessa Fleetwater; 12 days; August

Problem #56

Anthony Franklin; Wednesday; Friday
Barry Richardson; Friday; Monday
Denise Bellows; Tuesday; Tuesday
Larry Carlton; Monday; Wednesday
Natalie Ashcroft; Thursday; Thursday

Problem #57

Position 1; Linda Walters; Exception
Position 2; Kerrie Pancoe; Forecast
Position 3; Jason Bliss; Status
Position 4; Linda Smith; Progress

Problem #58

Position 1; Victor; Megan; Pictures
Position 2; Zoe; Bobbi; Toys
Position 3; Paul; Tommy; Foreign Coins
Position 4; Alice; Charlie; Clothes

Problem #59

Seat 1; George Franklin
Seat 2; Sue Gregory
Seat 3; Harriet Peck

Seat 4; Jordan Michaels
Seat 5; Theresa Carlton
Seat 6; Victor Harwood
Seat 7; Rebecca Newell
Seat 8; Adam Rim

Problem #60

Product A; Orange; Brown; Maroon
Product B; Green; Black; Beige
Product C; Red; Purple; Gray
Product D; Yellow; Blue; Olive

Problem #61

Position 1; Clarissa; Cost Escalations; $80K
Position 2; Barbara; Poor Coding; $50K
Position 3; Fred; Poor Quality; $60K
Position 4; George; Design Flaws; $30K

Problem #62

Position 1; Bryan; 5; 10
Position 2; Horace; 7; 14
Position 3; Carl; 8; 12
Position 4; Edward; 6; 18

Problem #63

Position 1; Andrea; Lack of Raw Materials
Position 2; Dora; Breakdown in Equipment
Position 3; Philip; Bad Weather
Position 4; John; Lack of Human Resources
Position 5; Emily; Wrong Skill Level of the Resources
Position 6; Thomas; Wrong Raw Materials
Position 7; Helen; Workers Out Sick

Problem #64

601; Dora Nullworth; VP Engineering
602; Fred Edgeworth; VP Accounting
603; Hubert Jenworth; President
604; Karl Pegworth; VP Manufacturing
605; Louis Woolworth; VP Human Relations
606; Conrad Hogsworth; Executive VP

607; Ethan Dilworth; Senior VP and Legal Counsel
608; Juliett Lensworth; VP Quality

Problem #65

Work Package 1; —; R; —; —
Work Package 2: R; C; I; A
Work Package 3; —; C; R; —
Work Package 4; R; —; A; I
Work Package 5; —; R; I; —

Problem #66

Activity A; $100; $200; $400
Activity B; $1000; $1100; $1200
Activity C; $300; $600; $500
Activity D; $800; $900; $700
Activity E; $1500; $1400; $1300

Problem #67

Position 1; Joseph; VP Information Systems; Uncle
Position 2; Jenny; President; Mother
Position 3; John; VP Engineering; Brother
Position 4; Jessica; VP Manufacturing; Sister
Position 5; Jane; VP Quality; Sister
Position 6; Jeff; VP Finance; Father

Problem #68

Position A; Bob; Prince Co.; 4 days
Position B; Adam; Swift Co.; 3 days
Position C; George; Wellington Co.; 2 days
Position D; Helen; Robertson Co.; 5 days

Problem #69

Position 1; Cordell; Managing Multiple Projects; 2nd
Position 2; Harriett; Quality Improvements; 6th
Position 3; Dell; Planning Skills; 4th
Position 4; Fiona; Ability to Work with People; 1st
Position 5; Gertrude; Cost Savings; 5th
Position 6; Thomas; Customer Satisfaction; 3rd

Problem #70

First Draw; Phyllis; 28th
Second Draw; Harry; 26th
Third Draw; Eddie; 29th
Fourth Draw; Willy; 31st
Fifth Draw; Grant; 27th
Sixth Draw; Paula; 30th

Problem #71

Seat 1; John; Project Manager; $35K
Seat 2; Ned; Executive Sponsor; $30K
Seat 3; Dolores; APM Cost; $25K
Seat 4; Paula; APM Quality; $20K

Problem #72

Position 1; Henry Ithica; Rollins Chemicals; Klein Project
Position 2; Edward Fogle; Paragon Chemicals; Newman Project
Position 3; Carol Demmings; Novelis Chemicals; Porthas Project
Position 4; Alex Baker; Aramis Chemicals; Jolliett Project

Problem #73

Position 1; Project Management Office; Neville Marsh; $60
Position 2; Risk Management; Jane Aston; $45
Position 3; Portfolio Management; Paul Wadsworth; $55
Position 4; Advanced Project Management; Peggy Frummel; $50

Problem #74

Office 302; Wally; Chicken; Cake
Office 304; Megan; Meat; Cookies
Office 306; Anthony; Stuffed Peppers; Assorted Cheeses
Office 308; Polly; Pasta; Ice Cream

Problem #75

Position 1; Archie Flowers; Richter
Position 2; Basil Evert; Pongo
Position 3; Denise Heinz; Triton
Position 4; Charlene Grant; Unger

Problem #76

Position 1; Forman Team; Five Stars; Red and White
Position 2; Rockwall Team; Crossed Swords; Green and Yellow
Position 3; Prentice Aerospace Team; Lightning Bolts; Black and Orange
Position 4; Maximillian Satellite Team; Wolf; Purple and Blue

Problem #77

Position 1; Caroline Hill; 23%
Position 2; Lucas Denton; 28%
Position 3; Kevin Atkins; 12%
Position 4; Lynn Harrison; 15%

Problem #78

Position 1; Johnson; Gumsy; Engineering
Position 2; Herkens; Urman; Procurement
Position 3; Guilliani; Billings; Quality
Position 4; James; Trundwell; Cost Control
Position 5; Caldwell; Harwood; Cost Estimating
Position 6; Anderson; Ray; Manufacturing

Problem #79

Position 1; Frank Pickler; 30
Position 2; Ingrid Graham; 60
Position 3; Paulette Froth; 120
Position 4; Gregory Daniels; 90

Problem #80

Booth 1; Avron Software Corp.; Flowers; Best Practices Libraries
Booth 2; Business Software Corp.; Blotto; EVMS
Booth 3; Future Software Co.; Tulip; Estimating
Booth 4; Easy-to-Use Software Co.; Iris; Scheduling

Problem #81

Anthony Ashcroft; 4 weeks of slippages; 5 meetings
Barry Bellows; 6; 8
Denise Richardson; 5; 4
Larry Franklin; 3; 16
Natalie Carlton; 2; 2

Problem #82

Conference room 1; George; Blue Company; 4 hours
Conference room 2; Howard; Grey Company; 3 hours
Conference room 3; Phillip; White Company; 5 hours
Conference room 4; Charles; Green Company; 2 hours

Problem #83

Drawer 1; Sandstone
Drawer 2; Castin
Drawer 3; Tennedyne
Drawer 4; Newton
Drawer 5; Magnoflex
Drawer 6; Delphino
Drawer 7; Eagle Products
Drawer 8; Coltex

Problem #84

Seat 1; Paul Troff; President
Seat 2; Carol Roth; Project Manager
Seat 3; Joseph Stedwell; VP Human Relations
Seat 4; Bob Phillips; VP Project Management

Problem #85

Position 1; Purple; 2006
Position 2; Red; 2005
Position 3; Brown; 2004
Position 4; Orange; 2002
Position 5; Yellow; 2003
Position 6; Black; 2000
Position 7; Green; 2001
Position 8; Blue; 1999

Problem #86

Position 1; Pasta; Pie; Coffee
Position 2; Fish; Cheese; Wine
Position 3; Steak; Fruit; Soda
Position 4; Chicken; Ice Cream; Tea

Problem #87

Seat 1; Paula Azure
Seat 2; Kevin Gustafson
Seat 3; Henry Maloney
Seat 4; Tara Robertson
Seat 5; Marcus West
Seat 6; Kenneth Merriman
Seat 7; George Anderson

Problem #88

Position 1; Lenny; Bonnie; 4th
Position 2; Neil; Carol; 1st
Position 3; Mickey; Zelda; 3rd
Position 4; Joseph; Selma; 2nd

Problem #89

Position A; 6:30 a.m.; *Learning from Project Disasters;* 2001
Position B; 6:00 a.m.; *Scheduling Techniques;* 2004
Position C; 7:00 a.m.; *Project Management Basics;* 2002
Position D; 7:30 a.m.; *Earned Value Management;* 2003
Position E; 6:15 a.m.; *Risk Management;* 2000

Problem #90

Position 1; New Product Development; Annette Prince; Alpha
Position 2; Cost Savings from Less Scrap; Brad Korman; Gamma
Position 3; Improved Quality in Manufacturing; Gabriel Lenso; Delta
Position 4; Customer Satisfaction; Chloe Radway; Zeta
Position 5; Higher Profit Margin; Inga Bickerson; Rho

Problem #91

Office 1; Carol; Pay Grade 9; 4 years
Office 2; David; Pay Grade 6; 2 years
Office 3; Edith; Pay Grade 8; 3 years
Office 4; Tom; Pay Grade 7; 1 year

Problem #92

Position 1; Jenett; *PM Universe*; April
Position 2; Davin; *World of Project Management*; June

Position 3; Sturgo; *Applied Project Management*; March
Position 4; Vitmar; *PM Success*; February
Position 5; Nethrow; *Management of Projects*; May

Problem #93

Space 1; Chevy; White
Space 2; Pontiac; Blue
Space 3; Toyota; Silver
Space 4; Mercury; Gray
Space 5; Buick; Black

Problem #94

Position 1; Manteen; 5; 4th
Position 2; Tribble; 13; 1st
Position 3; Green Filter; 2nd
Position 4; Klondike; 3rd

Problem #95

Position 1; Jerico; July; 14%
Position 2; Davis; June; 10%
Position 3; Hollingsworth; August; 16%
Position 4; Klontis; May; 12%

Problem #96

Position 1; Henry Carlsen; 700
Position 2; Elizabeth Dirkson; 451
Position 3; Mary Villano; 860
Position 4; Steven Netz; 489
Position 5; Fred Parker; 260
Position 6; Jordan Andrews; 590
Position 7; Nancy Storey; 285

Problem #97

Position 1; Brisco; Legal
Position 2; Watkins; Manufacturing
Position 3; Parsons; Procurement
Position 4; Nemens; Project Manager
Position 5; Flanagan; EVMS
Position 6; Yelling; Quality
Position 7; Kirchoff; Engineering

Problem #98

Position 1; Bryan Wallace; Vaporization
Position 2; Germain Spruce; Hot Gas
Position 3; Charles Tripp; Liquefaction
Position 4; April Morton; Cold Gas

Problem #99

Amos Front; 11; Watch
Bob Antine; 12; Plant
Darcy Barbo; 20; Radio
Karl Charpel; 19; Software
Mary Robertson; 16; Sweater

Problem #100

Space 1; Philip Corwin; Toyota
Space 2; Mary Germain; General Motors
Space 3; John Eagleton; Chrysler
Space 4; Larry Caster; Ford